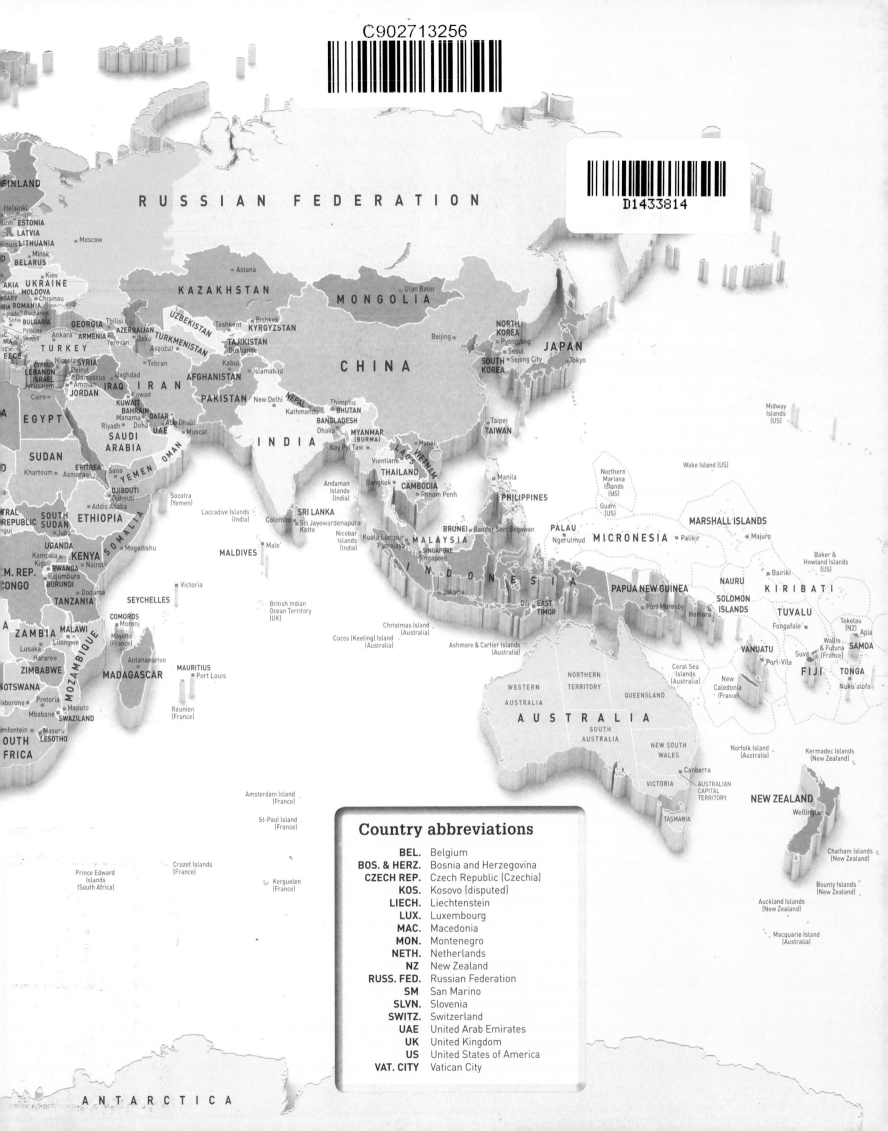

Country abbreviations

BEL.	Belgium
BOS. & HERZ.	Bosnia and Herzegovina
CZECH REP.	Czech Republic (Czechia)
KOS.	Kosovo (disputed)
LIECH.	Liechtenstein
LUX.	Luxembourg
MAC.	Macedonia
MON.	Montenegro
NETH.	Netherlands
NZ	New Zealand
RUSS. FED.	Russian Federation
SM	San Marino
SLVN.	Slovenia
SWITZ.	Switzerland
UAE	United Arab Emirates
UK	United Kingdom
US	United States of America
VAT. CITY	Vatican City

WHAT'S WEIRD
ON EARTH

DK

LONDON, NEW YORK, MUNICH,
MELBOURNE, and DELHI

Senior editors Fleur Star, Chris Hawkes
Senior art editor Rachael Grady

Editors Suhel Ahmed, Scarlett O'Hara, Vicky Richards
Designers David Ball, Chrissy Barnard, Sheila Collins,
Kit Lane, Sadie Thomas
3D illustrators Adam Benton, Simon Mumford
Illustrators Stuart Jackson-Carter, Jon @ KJA-Artists.com
Creative retouching Steve Crozier

Picture research Sumita Khatwani, Rituraj Singh,
Taiyaba Khatoon, Martin Copeland

Jacket design Mark Cavanagh
Jacket editor Claire Gell
Jacket design development manager
Sophia M Tampakopoulos Turner

Producer (pre-production) David Almond
Production controller Angela Graef

Managing art editor Philip Letsu
Managing editor Francesca Baines
Publisher Andrew Macintyre
Art director Karen Self
Associate publishing director Liz Wheeler
Publishing director Jonathan Metcalf

First published in Great Britain in 2018
by Dorling Kindersley Limited
80 Strand, London WC2R 0RL

A CIP catalogue record for this book
is available from the British Library.

ISBN: 978-0-2413-1762-4

Printed and bound in Hong Kong by Hung Hing

Discover more at
www.dk.com

CONTENTS

Nature

Supernatural

Bat-winged
lizard

Yeti

Hot lips
plant

Places

Meitan Tea Museum

People

Casu Marzu

History

Healthy hair

Fun facts

In Bulgaria and southern Albania, shaking your head from side to side means "yes".

Nature

Glowing caves
New Zealand's Waitomo Caves are lit up with glow-worms (the larvae of fungus gnats). The larvae spin traps of sticky threads and shine their blue tail-lights to lure in insects as prey.

Fly Geyser
Nevada, USA
These algae-covered geyser cones formed after water was struck during oil drilling.

Petrifying Well
Yorkshire, England
Objects placed in this well are turned to stone by dripping mineral water.

Cave of the Crystals
Naica, Mexico
Giant crystals, some more than 10 m (33 ft) long, grow in a deep cavern.

Ringing Rocks Park
Pennsylvania, USA
The rocks in this park make a musical ringing sound when struck with a hammer.

The Boiling River
Central Peruvian Amazon
Reaching temperatures above 93 °C (200 °F), this stretch of the Amazon river boils any animal that falls into it.

Salar de Uyuni
Bolivia
At 10,582 sq km (4,086 sq miles) this is the world's largest salt flat.

Fairy Circles
Namib Desert, Namibia
It is thought that these discs of bare red ground scattered over the desert are the work of termites.

Northern Lights
Seen in far northern night skies, these multi-coloured streams of light are caused by charged particles from the Sun colliding with Earth's atmospheric gases.

It takes 3–5 months to **turn** a **teddy bear** to **stone** in the **Petrifying Well** in Yorkshire, UK.

A SINGLE WAVE, 4 M (13 FT) HIGH, CALLED THE POROROCA ROLLS UP THE

Movile Cave
Constanta County, Romania
Strange creepy-crawlies thrive in this cave, which is full of poisonous gases.

Red Beach
Panjin, China
Rare grasses turn this marshland an unbelievably bright crimson.

Dead Sea
Israel/Jordan
The water here contains so much salt that swimmers can float without any effort.

Kawah Ijen Volcano
Java, Indonesia
Dissolved metals turn the crater lake of this volcano a vivid turquoise blue.

Chocolate Hills
Bohol, Philippines
In the dry season, hundreds of low, conical green hills on this island change to a rich chocolate brown.

Sulphur Lakes
Danakil Depression, Ethiopia
At this location, the hottest place on Earth, near-boiling springs deposit sulphur and minerals in colourful formations.

Morning Glory Clouds
Northern Australia
This rare cloud formation, like giant cotton-wool rolls, can extend for 1,000 km (620 miles).

Naturally weird

From rocks that ring like bells to bright red grass and rivers hot enough to boil a frog, there are some very strange things on Earth. Even scientists can't work out how some of them exist.

AMAZON RIVER TWICE A YEAR AS FAR AS 800 KM (500 MILES) INLAND.

7

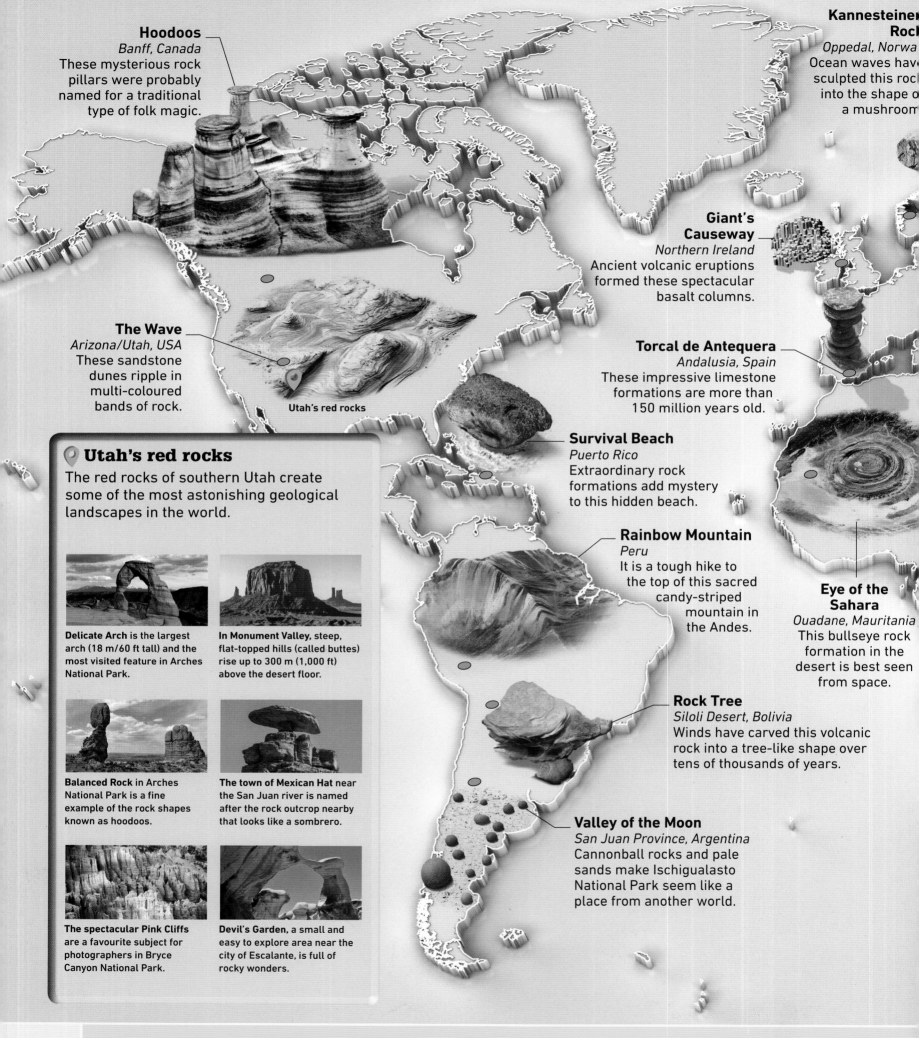

Hoodoos
Banff, Canada
These mysterious rock pillars were probably named for a traditional type of folk magic.

Kannesteinen Rock
Oppedal, Norway
Ocean waves have sculpted this rock into the shape of a mushroom

Giant's Causeway
Northern Ireland
Ancient volcanic eruptions formed these spectacular basalt columns.

The Wave
Arizona/Utah, USA
These sandstone dunes ripple in multi-coloured bands of rock.

Torcal de Antequera
Andalusia, Spain
These impressive limestone formations are more than 150 million years old.

Utah's red rocks

📍 Utah's red rocks

The red rocks of southern Utah create some of the most astonishing geological landscapes in the world.

Delicate Arch is the largest arch (18 m/60 ft tall) and the most visited feature in Arches National Park.

In Monument Valley, steep, flat-topped hills (called buttes) rise up to 300 m (1,000 ft) above the desert floor.

Balanced Rock in Arches National Park is a fine example of the rock shapes known as hoodoos.

The town of Mexican Hat near the San Juan river is named after the rock outcrop nearby that looks like a sombrero.

The spectacular Pink Cliffs are a favourite subject for photographers in Bryce Canyon National Park.

Devil's Garden, a small and easy to explore area near the city of Escalante, is full of rocky wonders.

Survival Beach
Puerto Rico
Extraordinary rock formations add mystery to this hidden beach.

Rainbow Mountain
Peru
It is a tough hike to the top of this sacred candy-striped mountain in the Andes.

Eye of the Sahara
Ouadane, Mauritania
This bullseye rock formation in the desert is best seen from space.

Rock Tree
Siloli Desert, Bolivia
Winds have carved this volcanic rock into a tree-like shape over tens of thousands of years.

Valley of the Moon
San Juan Province, Argentina
Cannonball rocks and pale sands make Ischigualasto National Park seem like a place from another world.

THE OLDEST ROCK FORMATIONS FOUND ON EARTH WERE

Kummakivi
Finland
This balancing stone was churned up by retreating glaciers at the end of the last Ice Age.

Manpupuner Rocks
Komi Republic, Russia
Seven vast standing stones, some more than 40 m (130 ft) tall, rear up from a grassy plateau.

Gansu Zhangye National Geopark
Northwest China
The sandstone formations in this national park are layered in beautiful paintbox colours.

Pravčická Brána *Czech Republic*
With a span of 25.5 m (87 ft) this is Europe's largest natural sandstone arch.

Krishna's Butterball
Mahabalipuram, India
This 6-m (20-ft) high boulder looks as though it's ready to roll away.

Immortal Bridge
Mount Tai, China
Three great boulders form a natural bridge above a deep ravine.

White Desert
Farafra, Egypt
e rocks in this desert are chalk-white in colour.

Queen's Head Rock *Taiwan*
This sea-worn rock is said to look like the profile of the Tudor Queen Elizabeth I of England.

Al Naslaa
Saudi Arabia
Split into two perfect halves, this huge standing stone is a geological puzzle.

Devil's Marbles
Northern Territory, Australia
Round granite stones, sacred to Australian Aboriginal people, are scattered across a wide, shallow valley.

Matobo Hills
Zimbabwe
These distinctive rock formations cover much of Zimbabwe.

Kunming Stone Forest
Yunnan Province, China
Limestone weathered over thousands of years formed a 400-sq km (155-sq mile) stone "forest".

Totem Pole *Tasmania*
This rock spire towers 65 m (213 ft) out of the sea.

Nature's sculptures

Not all great works of art are seen in museums and galleries. Around the world, beautiful, bizarre, and breathtaking rock sculptures have been created not with tools but by natural forces, such as wind and water, over huge stretches of time.

Moeraki Boulders
Otago, New Zealand
Amazingly, these large, round boulders, which lie on a beach, are hollow.

DISCOVERED IN CANADA AND DATE BACK NEARLY 4.3 BILLION YEARS.

9

Lost lake
Oregon, USA
This lake does a disappearing act each year, when it empties down a hole left by an old lava tube.

Longest-lasting lightning bolt
Côte d'Azur, France
On 30 August 2012, a single flash of lightning lasted for 7.74 seconds – the longest ever recorded.

Super outbreak *USA*
A series of tornadoes in April 2011 across the eastern half of the US was the largest and costliest ever. On 27 April alone, there were 199 tornadoes.

Beacon of Maracaibo
Venezuela
This area gets more lightning than anywhere else on Earth. There are strikes on 297 days every year, making it a very dangerous place to live.

Mount Washington
This peak in New Hampshire, USA, gets some extreme weather. There is not only heavy snow and freezing temperatures but also strong winds. At the summit, there is a building held down with heavy chains.

Penitentes
Argentina/Chile
These strange spiky ice or snow formations appear at high altitudes in the Andes Mountains. They can reach over 5 m (16 ft) high.

Unusual weather

Strange weather phenomena are found in places with similar conditions around the world. They may create beautiful icy shapes, or unusual cloud formations, or they may produce extreme storms, which are thankfully rare.

Ice circles form in slow-moving water in cold climates. The discs look like icy lily pads and can be up to 15 m (49 ft) across.

Twin tornadoes are unusual. They occur when two twisters from the same supercell touch the ground at the same time.

Inversion clouds appear much nearer the ground than usual, forming when a layer of cold air is trapped by a layer of warm air.

Rainiest place
Mawsynram, India
It rains a lot in the lush green hills of Mawsynram, a massive 11,862 mm (467 in) a year.

Coloured snow
Stavropol, Russia
The people of Stavropol, Russia, woke up to purple snow one morning in 2010. Dust carried by a cyclone from Africa had mixed with snow clouds over Russia.

Deepest snowfall
Mount Ibuki, Japan
During 1927, a huge 1,182 cm (465½ in) of snow was dumped on Mount Ibuki in Japan.

Hottest inhabited place
Dallol, Ethiopia Boiling hot and bone dry, this is a very difficult place to live. If this wasn't bad enough, there is also lots of volcanic activity here.

Sea foam
Lorne, Australia
A gigantic natural bubble bath with foam up to 1.8 m (6 ft) high formed along the coast here in 2012.

Wild weather

Moonbows
Victoria Falls, Zambia/ Zimbabwe
When moonlight shines through the spray from Victoria Falls it creates a silvery moonbow.

Talking about the weather will never be boring again with these record-breaking weather events and unusual climatic phenomena. Some conditions are strange and beautiful, but others can be deadly.

[-135.8 °F]. IT WAS MEASURED IN EAST ANTARCTICA IN AUGUST 2010.

11

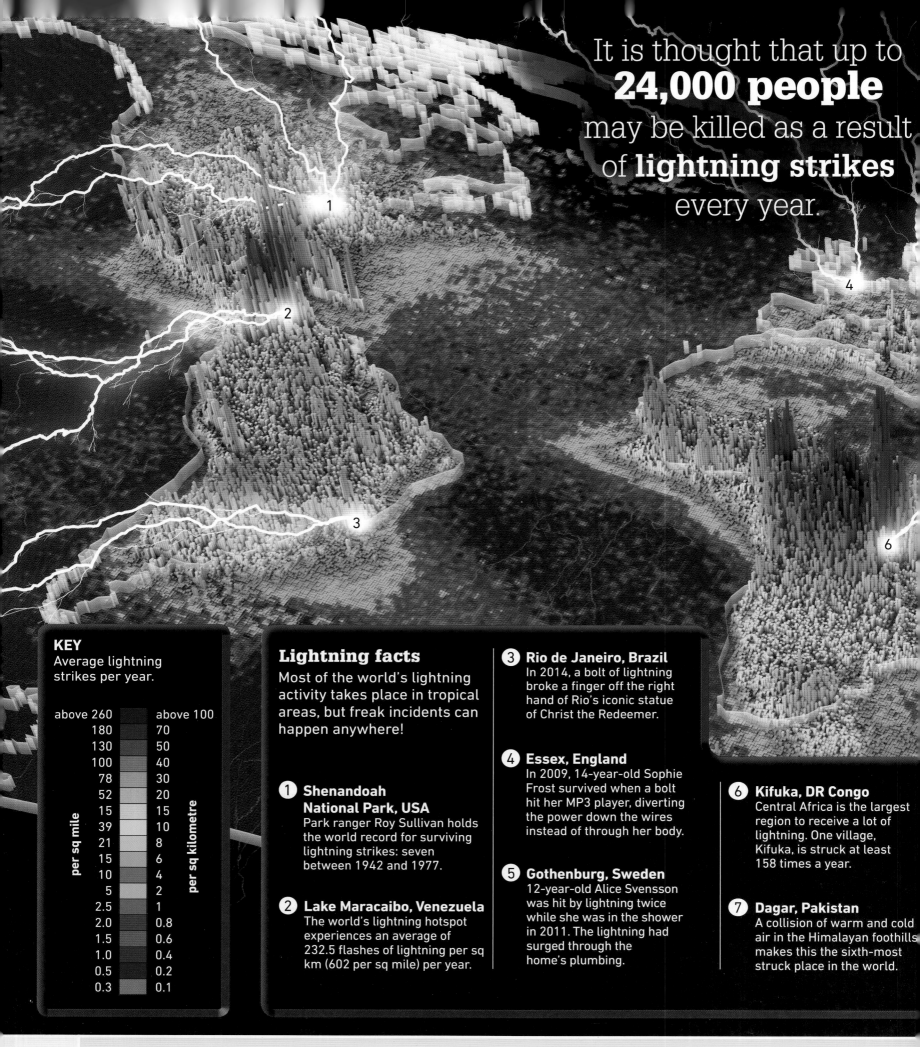

It is thought that up to **24,000 people** may be killed as a result of **lightning strikes** every year.

KEY
Average lightning strikes per year.

per sq mile		per sq kilometre
above 260		above 100
180		70
130		50
100		40
78		30
52		20
15		15
39		10
21		8
15		6
10		4
5		2
2.5		1
2.0		0.8
1.5		0.6
1.0		0.4
0.5		0.2
0.3		0.1

Lightning facts

Most of the world's lightning activity takes place in tropical areas, but freak incidents can happen anywhere!

① Shenandoah National Park, USA
Park ranger Roy Sullivan holds the world record for surviving lightning strikes: seven between 1942 and 1977.

② Lake Maracaibo, Venezuela
The world's lightning hotspot experiences an average of 232.5 flashes of lightning per sq km (602 per sq mile) per year.

③ Rio de Janeiro, Brazil
In 2014, a bolt of lightning broke a finger off the right hand of Rio's iconic statue of Christ the Redeemer.

④ Essex, England
In 2009, 14-year-old Sophie Frost survived when a bolt hit her MP3 player, diverting the power down the wires instead of through her body.

⑤ Gothenburg, Sweden
12-year-old Alice Svensson was hit by lightning twice while she was in the shower in 2011. The lightning had surged through the home's plumbing.

⑥ Kifuka, DR Congo
Central Africa is the largest region to receive a lot of lightning. One village, Kifuka, is struck at least 158 times a year.

⑦ Dagar, Pakistan
A collision of warm and cold air in the Himalayan foothills makes this the sixth-most struck place in the world.

Lightning strikes

This map shows the frequency of lightning strikes around the world. Areas in warmer, tropical climates (close to the Equator), and those in the region of large mountain ranges (such as the Andes and Himalayas), are the most susceptible.

8 Indonesia
The mountain ranges in the Indonesian islands of Java and Sumatra's are hotspots for lightning.

9 Malabar, Australia
Unfortunate Joanne Nitscke has had her house struck three times by lightning in 20 years – this happened even though she moved homes during that time.

AVERAGE OF 297 DAYS EVERY YEAR WITH LIGHTNING ACTIVITY.

Eyjafjallajökull erupts

This ice-topped volcano had been dormant for more than 180 years before it erupted in 2010. After a small initial eruption in March, an explosion near the summit on 14 April created a plume of ash more than 10 km (6⅕ miles) high. Over the following days and months, the ash created an enormous cloud that spread across the globe.

14 April, 12pm
By midday on the day of the eruption, the ash cloud was already drifting east.

14 April, 6pm
By the evening, the cloud had drifted further into European airspace.

18 April, 6am
By this point, the cloud had spread across most of Europe and into eastern Russia.

No-fly zone
The ash cloud contained thousands of tiny particles of volcanic rock, which, it was thought, could affect aircraft engines. Around 75 per cent of all European flights were cancelled as a safety precaution.

Cloud base
As the cloud reached a temporary peak on 18 April, scientists estimated that the volcano was ejecting 750 tonnes of magma (hot liquid rock) every single second.

ICELAND

EUROPE

Mediterranean Sea

THE ERUPTION LEFT MORE THAN 10 MILLION PEOPLE

5 April, 6am
The following day the cloud was over parts of the UK and Scandinavia.

16 April, 6am
Two days after the eruption, flights began to be significantly affected.

17 April, 6am
Three days after the eruption, the cloud covered most of northern Europe.

Eruption disruption

In April 2010, planes were grounded as an enormous cloud of ash swept across Europe. Shown here at one of its worst moments, on 18 April, the cloud continued to drift across the globe for the next few months – with parts of it even reaching as far as the eastern coast of America, northern Africa, and northeast Asia.

Knock-on effect
With most European airports shut, 30 per cent of all flights in Africa were also cancelled, along with 20 per cent of those in the Middle East.

ASIA

Icelandic volcanoes
Iceland is home to more than one hundred volcanoes, with 30 or more of these thought to be active. Although the eruption of Eyjafjallajökull was highly disruptive, it is actually one of the island's smaller volcanoes.

STRANDED AND COST AIRLINES A TOTAL OF US$1.7 BILLION.

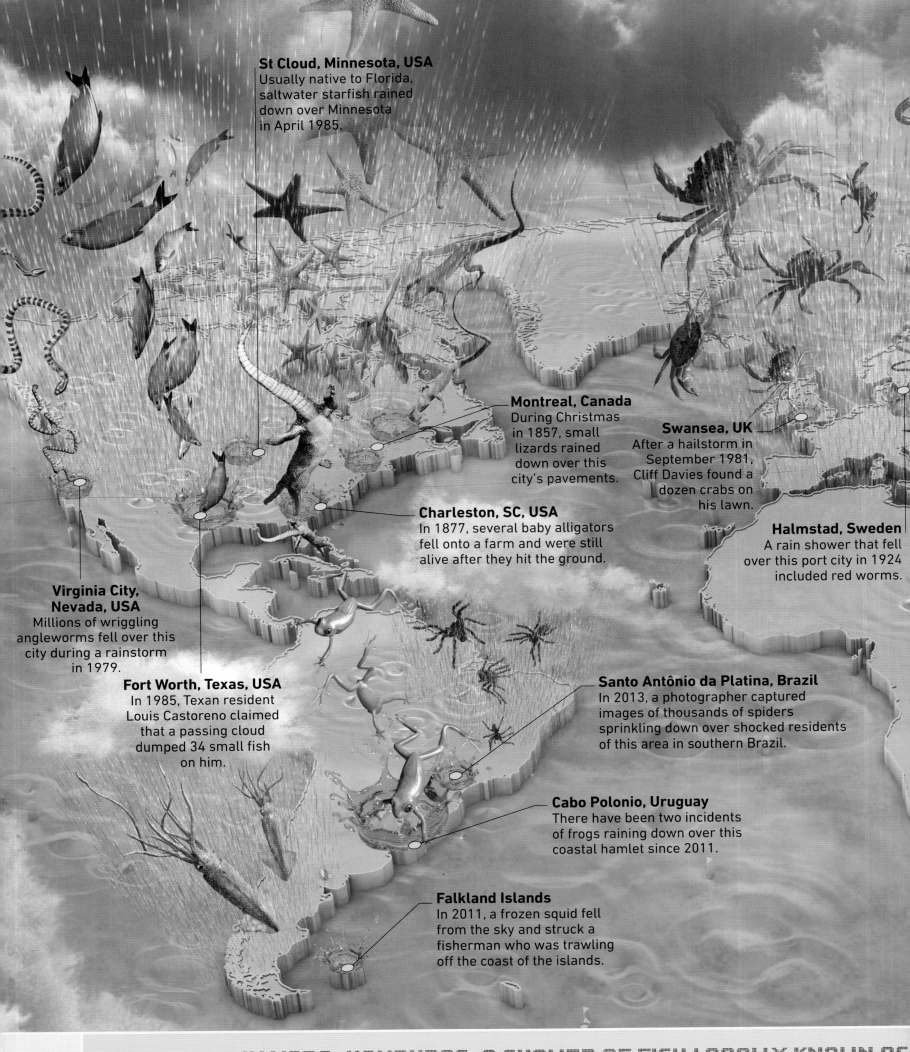

St Cloud, Minnesota, USA
Usually native to Florida, saltwater starfish rained down over Minnesota in April 1985.

Montreal, Canada
During Christmas in 1857, small lizards rained down over this city's pavements.

Swansea, UK
After a hailstorm in September 1981, Cliff Davies found a dozen crabs on his lawn.

Halmstad, Sweden
A rain shower that fell over this port city in 1924 included red worms.

Charleston, SC, USA
In 1877, several baby alligators fell onto a farm and were still alive after they hit the ground.

Virginia City, Nevada, USA
Millions of wriggling angleworms fell over this city during a rainstorm in 1979.

Fort Worth, Texas, USA
In 1985, Texan resident Louis Castoreno claimed that a passing cloud dumped 34 small fish on him.

Santo Antônio da Platina, Brazil
In 2013, a photographer captured images of thousands of spiders sprinkling down over shocked residents of this area in southern Brazil.

Cabo Polonio, Uruguay
There have been two incidents of frogs raining down over this coastal hamlet since 2011.

Falkland Islands
In 2011, a frozen squid fell from the sky and struck a fisherman who was trawling off the coast of the islands.

IN YORO, HONDURAS, A SHOWER OF FISH LOCALLY KNOWN AS

Pokroff, Russia
A shower of insects with flat, shiny heads fell over this Russian town in 1827.

How does it happen?
Animal showers are most likely caused by waterspouts that form over the sea during storms and suck up marine life. The animals are then carried over land and when the wind drops they fall to the ground.

Madhesh, Nepal
Small fish fell over this village in May 1900.

Kandanassery, India
A downpour over this village in 2008 included thousands of small fish.

Singapore
In 1861, a shower of fish fell in the city-state during three days of torrential rain.

Rákóczifalva, Hungary
In 2010, residents of this town were stunned when a thunderstorm brought down a shower of frogs.

Dire Dawa, Ethiopia
In 2000, the people of this city thought a shower of fish that lasted several minutes was a divine blessing.

Raining animals

Lombok, Indonesia
In 1969, farmers saw rats fall from the sky and then scatter across the fields.

Animals raining down on Earth may sound like the stuff of fiction, but it actually happens in real life. In fact, reports of animals mysteriously falling out of the sky abound throughout the world.

Lajamanu, Australia
Hundreds of fish bombarded residents of this outback town in 2010.

Goulburn, Australia
Millions of tiny spiders fell over the New South Wales countryside in 2015 and blanketed the area with their webs.

"LLUVIA DE PECES" OCCURS BETWEEN MAY AND JULY EVERY YEAR.

Grand Prismatic Spring
Wyoming, USA
Found in Yellowstone National Park, this multi-coloured marvel is deeper than a 10-storey building.

Spotted Lake
British Columbia, Canada
Most of this lake crystallizes in summer, leaving behind large spots of water.

Horsetail Fall
California, USA
At sunset from the end of February, the Sun's light hits this waterfall at such an angle that it makes the water look like a stream of fire.

Rio Tinto
Andalusia, Spain
It's best to avoid this red river. Years of mining have filled it with highly acidic minerals.

La Brea Pitch Lake
Trinidad and Tobago
This is the largest lake in the world made of pitch, or tar – a natural sticky black substance that has many uses.

Caño Cristales
La Macarena, Colombia
Little aquatic plants cause this river to turn a shocking red colour. Known as the "liquid rainbow", it also contains patches of yellow, green, orange, and blue.

Lake Retba
Dakar, Senegal
Tiny bacteria cause this lake's vivid pink colour. They are attracted to its high salt content.

Laguna Colorada
Potosí, Bolivia
This blood-red lake is home to a rare species of flamingo.

Weird water

From pink pools to lime-green lakes, the water of the world comes in a wonderful variety of weird colours. These brilliant hues are usually caused by plants, bacteria, or natural minerals from the ground below.

KEY
The coloured frame surrounding each image shows what has caused the water's colour.

- Colour caused by minerals
- Colour caused by algae or bacteria
- Other reasons for colour

Rainbow beaches

It's not just water that can change colour; many shorelines can be found in surprising shades, too. From dark purple to eerie white, beaches around the world can be found in a variety of unexpected colours. Many are tourist hotspots, with eager visitors flocking in large numbers to see these unusual seashores.

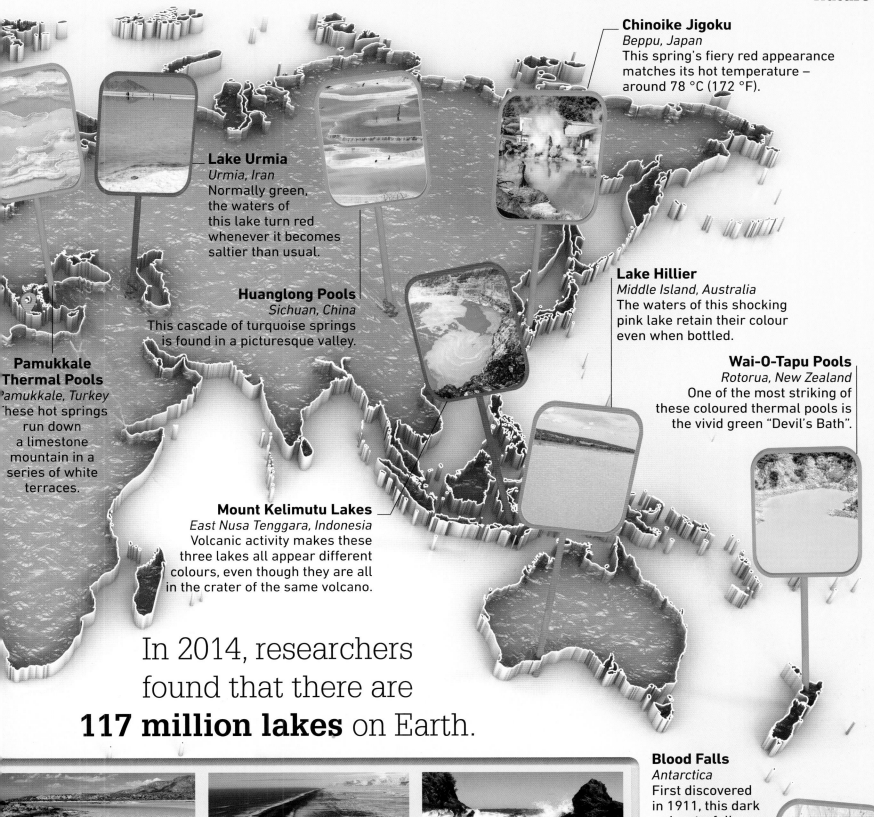

Chinoike Jigoku
Beppu, Japan
This spring's fiery red appearance matches its hot temperature – around 78 °C (172 °F).

Lake Urmia
Urmia, Iran
Normally green, the waters of this lake turn red whenever it becomes saltier than usual.

Lake Hillier
Middle Island, Australia
The waters of this shocking pink lake retain their colour even when bottled.

Huanglong Pools
Sichuan, China
This cascade of turquoise springs is found in a picturesque valley.

Pamukkale Thermal Pools
Pamukkale, Turkey
These hot springs run down a limestone mountain in a series of white terraces.

Wai-O-Tapu Pools
Rotorua, New Zealand
One of the most striking of these coloured thermal pools is the vivid green "Devil's Bath".

Mount Kelimutu Lakes
East Nusa Tenggara, Indonesia
Volcanic activity makes these three lakes all appear different colours, even though they are all in the crater of the same volcano.

In 2014, researchers found that there are **117 million lakes** on Earth.

Blood Falls
Antarctica
First discovered in 1911, this dark red waterfall stands out sharply against the white ice.

Elafonisi beach in Crete has patches of stunning pink sand along its normally white shore. Crushed coral and seashells give the sand this unusual colour.

Several black sand beaches are found near the town of Vik in Iceland. They are made up of tiny particles of a volcanic rock called basalt.

Kaihalulu beach in Maui, Hawaii, USA, is one of many colourful beaches on the island. The high iron content of the surrounding hills makes the sand appear bright red.

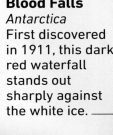

Drifting ducks

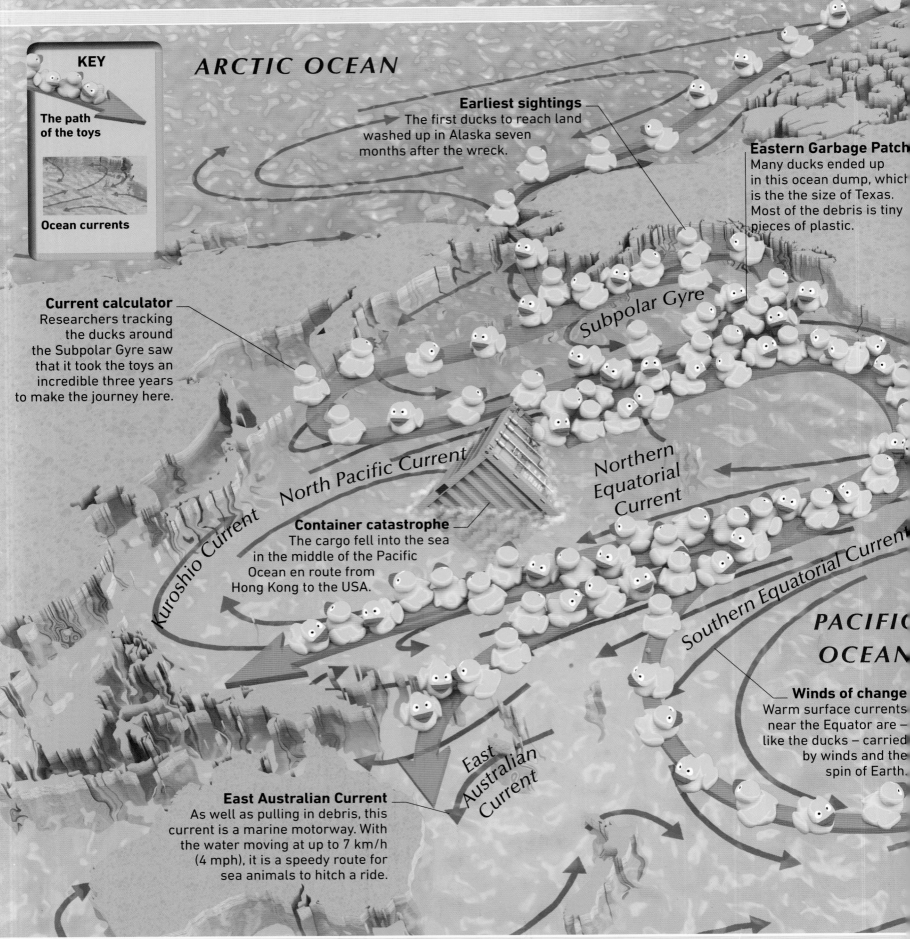

ARCTIC OCEAN

KEY

The path of the toys

Ocean currents

Earliest sightings
The first ducks to reach land washed up in Alaska seven months after the wreck.

Eastern Garbage Patch
Many ducks ended up in this ocean dump, which is the the size of Texas. Most of the debris is tiny pieces of plastic.

Current calculator
Researchers tracking the ducks around the Subpolar Gyre saw that it took the toys an incredible three years to make the journey here.

Subpolar Gyre

North Pacific Current

Northern Equatorial Current

Kuroshio Current

Container catastrophe
The cargo fell into the sea in the middle of the Pacific Ocean en route from Hong Kong to the USA.

Southern Equatorial Current

PACIFIC OCEAN

Winds of change
Warm surface currents near the Equator are — like the ducks — carried by winds and the spin of Earth.

East Australian Current

East Australian Current
As well as pulling in debris, this current is a marine motorway. With the water moving at up to 7 km/h (4 mph), it is a speedy route for sea animals to hitch a ride.

IT'S THOUGHT THAT BETWEEN 2,000 AND 10,000 CONTAINERS

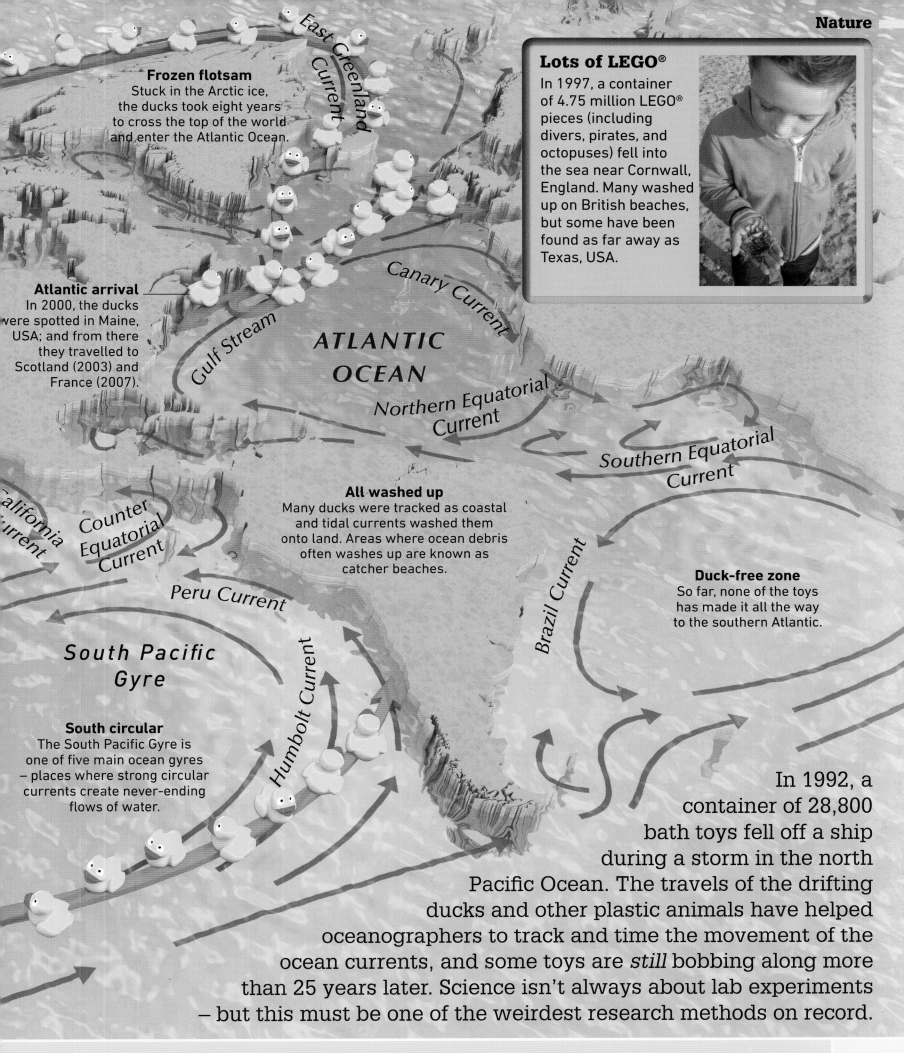

Frozen flotsam
Stuck in the Arctic ice, the ducks took eight years to cross the top of the world and enter the Atlantic Ocean.

East Greenland Current

Lots of LEGO®
In 1997, a container of 4.75 million LEGO® pieces (including divers, pirates, and octopuses) fell into the sea near Cornwall, England. Many washed up on British beaches, but some have been found as far away as Texas, USA.

Atlantic arrival
In 2000, the ducks were spotted in Maine, USA; and from there they travelled to Scotland (2003) and France (2007).

Canary Current

Gulf Stream

ATLANTIC
OCEAN

Northern Equatorial Current

Southern Equatorial Current

California Current

Counter Equatorial Current

All washed up
Many ducks were tracked as coastal and tidal currents washed them onto land. Areas where ocean debris often washes up are known as catcher beaches.

Brazil Current

Peru Current

Duck-free zone
So far, none of the toys has made it all the way to the southern Atlantic.

South Pacific Gyre

Humbolt Current

South circular
The South Pacific Gyre is one of five main ocean gyres – places where strong circular currents create never-ending flows of water.

In 1992, a container of 28,800 bath toys fell off a ship during a storm in the north Pacific Ocean. The travels of the drifting ducks and other plastic animals have helped oceanographers to track and time the movement of the ocean currents, and some toys are *still* bobbing along more than 25 years later. Science isn't always about lab experiments – but this must be one of the weirdest research methods on record.

At one with nature

The following animals are masters of camouflage. They can disguise themselves as leaves or sticks, tricking predator and prey alike.

The pink-and-white orchid mantis, in Borneo, conceals itself in an orchid petal as it waits for its prey.

Leaf insects, found in many regions, are sometimes called "walking leaves", as they look like just that!

The giant prickly stick insect uses its colouring and unusual shape to hide among sticks and dry leaves.

Underwing moth
USA, Europe
The moth's first set of wings look like tree bark. Its second, coloured set is visible when it spreads its wings.

Flounder
Atlantic and North Pacific oceans
When this pale-coloured flatfish lies on the ocean floor, it blends in with the sand.

Comma butterf[ly]
Europe, As[ia], North Americ[a]
When th[e] butterfly's wing[s] are closed, it loo[ks] just like a dried lea[f]

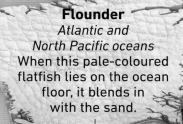

Goldenrod crab spider
North America, Europe
To catch its prey, this spider conceals itself in flowers by changing its colour to white or yellow.

Dynastor butterfly
Trinidad
The chrysalis of the *Darius Darius* species not only looks like a snake, it can also shake to suggest a moving snake.

Caribbean reef squid
Caribbean Sea
Using special skin cells, this squid can change colour to match its ocean background.

Glass frog
Central and South America
With green skin on its back and a transparent underside, predators see straight through this frog when it's on a leaf.

Sidewinding adder
Namibia, Angola
This venomous snake hides in the sand, its scales blending in, ready to snatch its prey.

Snake surprise

The atlas moth, found in Southeast Asia, also known as the "snake's head moth", has a pattern on its wings that looks just like a snake's head. To ward off threats, the moth flaps its wings, imitating a snake's head and neck.

The atlas moth's wing pattern resembles the venomous cobra, a type of snake found in Asia.

Atlas moth

Indian cobra

BLACK-AND-YELLOW HOVERFLIES LOOK SIMILAR TO WASPS. THEY HAVE

Arctic fox
Arctic region
With its white fur, this fox easily hides in the Arctic winter snow.

Asian swallowtail caterpillar
Asia and Hawaii, USA
When small, this caterpillar's colouring resembles bird poo – putting off any hungry predators.

Dead leaf butterfly
Southeast Asia
The underside of this brightly coloured butterfly resembles a dull brown leaf.

Gliding lizard
Southeast Asia
This reptile's skin is coloured like tree bark.

Common baron caterpillar
Southeast and South Asia
This caterpillar's green, spiny body looks like the leaves of the mango trees in which it lives.

Lacy scorpionfish
Indian and Pacific oceans
The patterned skin and unusual shape of this rare and venomous fish blend into its coral reef surroundings.

Satanic leaf-tailed gecko
Madagascar
This tiny lizard looks so much like a dry leaf, predators may overlook it.

Mimic octopus
Indo-Pacific region
This octopus is able to change both colour and shape to mimic other sea creatures – here a starfish.

Chameleon
Africa, Madagascar, Southern Europe, South Asia
Chameleons are famous for changing colour to display their moods.

Reef stonefish
Indo-Pacific region
The mottled skin of this extremely venomous fish makes it look like a stone on the ocean floor.

Animal camouflage

Whether to escape predators or lure in prey, these crafty creatures know how to keep well hidden. Across the globe, colour-changing and shape-shifting animals use their natural talents to keep either hidden, disguised, or alive.

Giant cuttlefish
Coastal waters of southern Australia
Cuttlefish can change colour instantly. They can also change their shape to resemble seaweed, rock, or sand.

Leafy sea-dragon
Coastal waters of southern Australia
Covered in leaf-like frills, this fish blends in perfectly with the surrounding seaweed.

Alaskan wood frog
Alaska, USA
Able to withstand extremely low temperatures, this population of frogs can survive even if two-thirds of the water in their body is frozen.

London Underground mosquito
London, England
Living in train tunnels, these insects have evolved to feed on humans and rats.

Star-nosed mole
Northeastern USA, Canada
This creature's star-shaped nose sends instant information to its brain, making it one of the fastest foragers on Earth.

Spotted salamander
Eastern USA, Canada
This secretive amphibian's embryos produce food in the same way as plants – by photosynthesis.

Mint-sauce worm
Atlantic Ocean
These social creatures have algae living inside them. They can make food by basking in the Sun.

Fennec fox
Sahara Desert, North Africa
This furry fox's large ears help keep it cool. They radiate the fox's body heat into the atmosphere.

Zombie worm
Pacific Ocean, North and Mediterranean seas
This creature has an unusual diet – whale bones. It releases a sticky acid to dissolve the bones so it can access their nutrients.

Giant tube worms
Eastern Pacific Ocean
With no digestive system of their own, these weird worms rely on bacteria living inside them to make their food.

Golden poison frog
Colombia
This toxic frog has enough poison inside it to kill 10 adult men.

Maned wolf
Central and Eastern South America
Long legs help these wolves roam over high grassland. They can also rotate their ears to better hear prey.

Glass sponge
Southern and Western Pacific oceans
Made out of silica – the same material used to make glass – these sponges can transmit light around their bodies, which may help them grow.

Chilean basket star
Chilean fjords
This marine animal uses its long, waving arms to hunt. It forms a basket in which it captures tiny sea creatures called krill.

Sea pig
Southern Ocean
These transparent scavengers search the sea floor for fallen food from above.

Antarctic icefish
Southern Ocean
This fish has a type of anti-freeze in its blood to prevent itself from freezing in its chilly habitat.

THE ONLY KNOWN ANIMALS THAT CAN SURVIVE IN OPEN

Poison frogs

The bright colours of these frogs aren't just for show. They warn predators that the frogs are extremely poisonous. Many other frogs imitate their colouring so that animals will also avoid them.

The Blue-jeans frog is named for its distinctive blue legs.

This Harlequin poison dart frog lives on the floor of tropical rainforests.

Blue poison dart frogs can live for around four to six years in the wild.

Olm
Slovenia, Croatia
This blind, cave-dwelling salamander can detect light through its skin.

Bactrian camel
Central and East Asia
The fatty humps of this desert dweller allow it to survive temperatures ranging from -28 °C (18 °F) to more than 38 °C (100 °F).

Sunda flying lemur
South East Asia
A large skin flap enables this animal to glide through the treetops.

Cassowary
New Guinea, Australia
This flightless bird has adapted to feed on a fruit that is toxic to most animals – the Cassowary plum.

Okapi
Central Africa
It is believed these mammals make calls to their young at a frequency predators cannot hear.

African bull frog *Africa*
This frog avoids droughts by hibernating in a moist sac for many months or even years, only emerging when rain comes.

Animal adaptations

Millions of years of evolution have placed many animals one step ahead of their environment. These adaptations allow them to survive in the most extreme habitats – from the deserts to the deep sea.

Thorny devil
Australia
Living in dry conditions, this spiky lizard can catch water in the gaps between its scales.

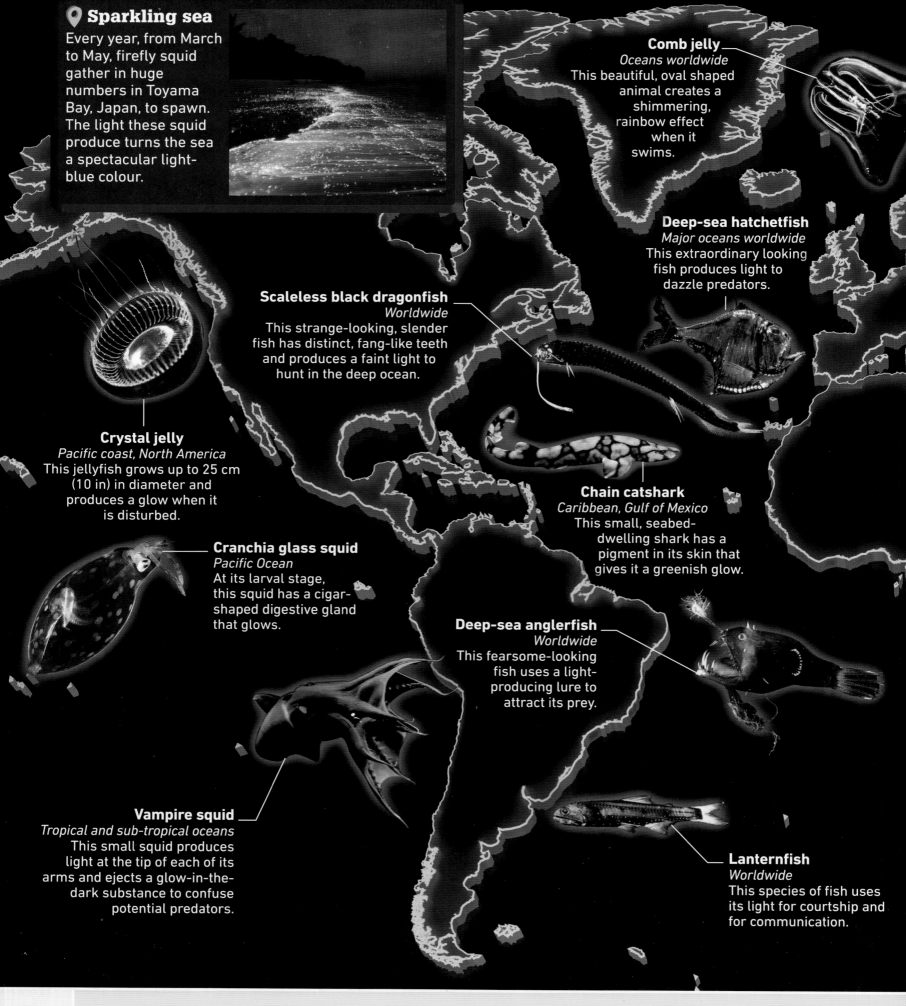

Every year, from March to May, firefly squid gather in huge numbers in Toyama Bay, Japan, to spawn. The light these squid produce turns the sea a spectacular light-blue colour.

Comb jelly
Oceans worldwide
This beautiful, oval shaped animal creates a shimmering, rainbow effect when it swims.

Deep-sea hatchetfish
Major oceans worldwide
This extraordinary looking fish produces light to dazzle predators.

Scaleless black dragonfish
Worldwide
This strange-looking, slender fish has distinct, fang-like teeth and produces a faint light to hunt in the deep ocean.

Crystal jelly
Pacific coast, North America
This jellyfish grows up to 25 cm (10 in) in diameter and produces a glow when it is disturbed.

Chain catshark
Caribbean, Gulf of Mexico
This small, seabed-dwelling shark has a pigment in its skin that gives it a greenish glow.

Cranchia glass squid
Pacific Ocean
At its larval stage, this squid has a cigar-shaped digestive gland that glows.

Deep-sea anglerfish
Worldwide
This fearsome-looking fish uses a light-producing lure to attract its prey.

Vampire squid
Tropical and sub-tropical oceans
This small squid produces light at the tip of each of its arms and ejects a glow-in-the-dark substance to confuse potential predators.

Lanternfish
Worldwide
This species of fish uses its light for courtship and for communication.

Glow-in-the-dark land animals

Although most light-producing animals live in the world's oceans, there are a few land animals, mostly insects, that are capable of producing light.

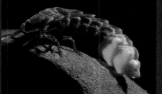

Some insect larvae, collectively known as glow-worms, have the ability to produce light.

Synchronous fireflies coordinate their "flashes". They turn them on and off at the same time.

The larva of the *Phrixothrix* beetle glows a green colour and is called the railroad worm.

Only a small number of the 12,000 known millipede species are able to produce light.

Firefly squid
Western Pacific Ocean
This small squid produces a deep-blue light to hide from predators against sunlit waters, and also for courtship.

Mantis shrimp
Indian and Pacific oceans
Certain species of this shrimp are fluorescent.

Toyama Bay
Japan

Pygmy shark
Oceans worldwide
This shark makes its belly glow to disguise itself against the sunlit ocean surface.

Neon animals

Travel down to the dark depths of the deep ocean and you're likely to witness one of nature's great light shows. About 80 per cent of the world's light-producing creatures live in the ocean.

Mountain goat
Rocky Mountains, Canada and USA
The great climbers of the natural world, these goats can climb seemingly impossibly steep slopes.

Hooded seal
North Atlantic and Arctic oceans
To attract a mate or to scare off rivals, male seals inflate a flap of skin on their nose that looks like a pink balloon.

Dung beetle
Africa, Europe, Asia
This beetle can bury a ball of dung 250 times heavier than itself in one night.

Texas horned lizard
Southern USA, Mexico
When threatened, this small desert lizard squirts blood from the corner of its eyes.

Tree goat
Morocco, Africa
These tree-climbing goats scale branches up to 10 m (33 ft) high to eat the fruit of the argan tree.

Solenodon
Cuba, Dominican Republic, Haiti
This small, shrew-like animal is one of only a few mammals to have a venomous bite.

Epomis beetle
Africa, Europe, Asia
This beetle's larvae cling to large amphibians, such as frogs, and start eating them.

Electric eel
Amazon and Orinoco rivers
To stun prey, these eels unleash up to 600 volts of electricity. That's five times more powerful than a standard US wall socket.

Green basilisk lizard
Central America
Found in rainforests, this lizard can run on water to escape predators.

Gerenuk
Horn of Africa
This member of the antelope family stands on its hind legs to reach leaves 1.8–2.4 m (6–8 ft) off the ground.

Three-toed sloth
Central and South America
This tree-dwelling animal moves so slowly that algae grows on its furry coat.

Decorator crabs
The fancy-dress lovers of the natural world, these crabs decorate themselves with seaweed, sponges, and anenomes. But it is not just for show: these decorations provide vital protection from predators.

Sponge decorator crab

Orangutan crab

Decorator crab with anemones

PUFFER FISH CONTAIN A TOXIN CALLED TETRODOTOXIN, WHICH IS

Beastly behaviour

From poisonous bites and electric shocks to extraordinary feats of lifting, climbing, flying, and even inflating, animals have developed a huge number of different behaviours and defence mechanisms.

Siberian salamander
Arctic, Northern Europe, Asia
This amphibian can survive in very low temperatures by deep-freezing itself until temperatures start to rise.

Irrawaddy dolphin
Southeast Asia
Found mostly in estuaries, many fishermen have told stories of how these dolphins help by guiding fish into fishing nets.

Puffer fish
Tropical and subtropical waters worldwide
As a defence, these fish consume huge amounts of water and turn into a virtually inedible ball.

Hardwicke's woolly bat
Southeast Asia
These bats have an extraordinary relationship with pitcher plants. In return for shelter, the bats poo in the plant, providing it with essential nitrogen.

Coconut crab
Islands across Indian and Pacific oceans
These huge crabs measure up to 1 m (3 ft) long and can break open coconut shells with their pincers.

Sea bunny
Indian and Pacific oceans
These sea slugs may look cute, but they have highly toxic skin to protect them from predators.

Wombat
Australia
These creatures produce cube-shaped pellets to mark their territory; round ones might roll away.

Mudskipper
Coastal waters of Indian and Pacific oceans
These amphibious fish can climb, walk, and skip about out of the water.

Blobfish
Coastal waters off Australia
These fish have very little muscle. They drift around the ocean at depths of 600–1,200 m (2,000–4,000 ft) eating whatever floats in front of them.

Flying fish
Warm oceans worldwide
To escape from predators, these fish leap out of the water and use their wing-like pectoral fins to fly through the air.

ABOUT 1,000 TIMES MORE POISONOUS THAN CYANIDE.

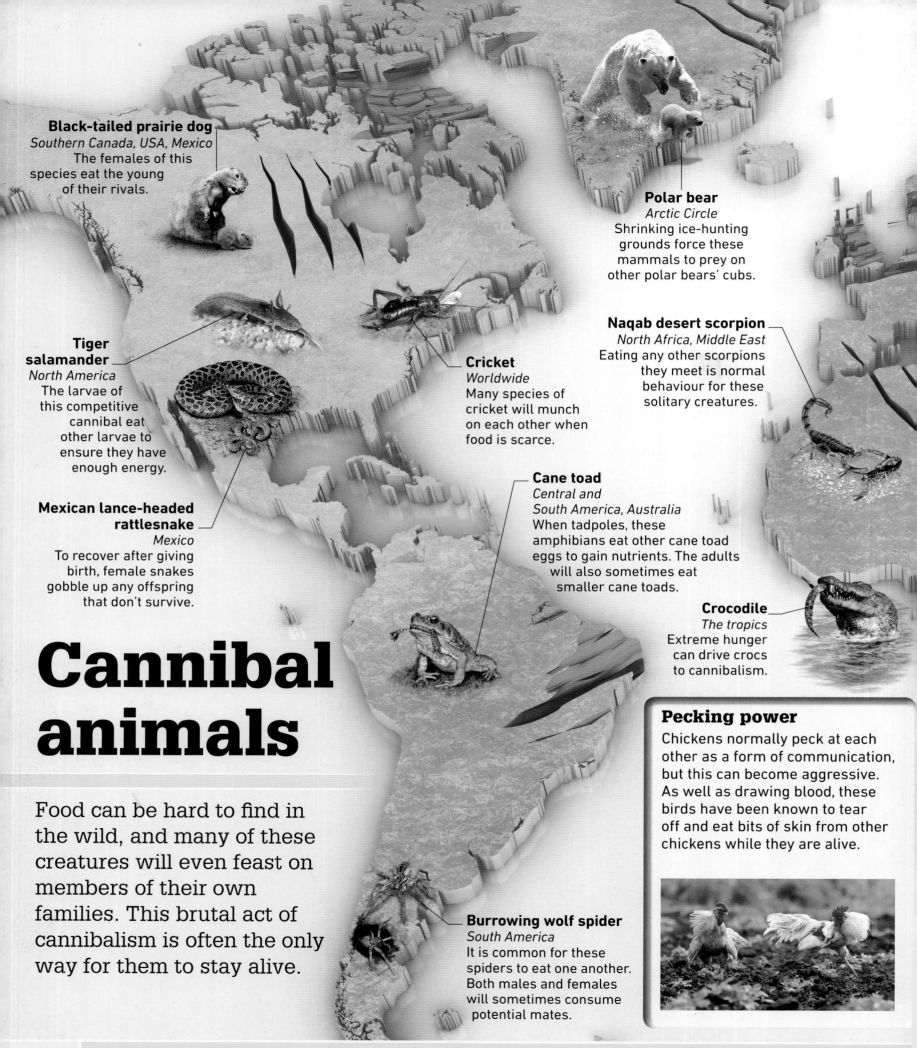

Cannibal animals

Food can be hard to find in the wild, and many of these creatures will even feast on members of their own families. This brutal act of cannibalism is often the only way for them to stay alive.

Black-tailed prairie dog
Southern Canada, USA, Mexico
The females of this species eat the young of their rivals.

Tiger salamander
North America
The larvae of this competitive cannibal eat other larvae to ensure they have enough energy.

Mexican lance-headed rattlesnake
Mexico
To recover after giving birth, female snakes gobble up any offspring that don't survive.

Polar bear
Arctic Circle
Shrinking ice-hunting grounds force these mammals to prey on other polar bears' cubs.

Cricket
Worldwide
Many species of cricket will munch on each other when food is scarce.

Naqab desert scorpion
North Africa, Middle East
Eating any other scorpions they meet is normal behaviour for these solitary creatures.

Cane toad
Central and South America, Australia
When tadpoles, these amphibians eat other cane toad eggs to gain nutrients. The adults will also sometimes eat smaller cane toads.

Crocodile
The tropics
Extreme hunger can drive crocs to cannibalism.

Burrowing wolf spider
South America
It is common for these spiders to eat one another. Both males and females will sometimes consume potential mates.

Pecking power

Chickens normally peck at each other as a form of communication, but this can become aggressive. As well as drawing blood, these birds have been known to tear off and eat bits of skin from other chickens while they are alive.

ALTHOUGH IT IS UNUSUAL, SOME ANIMALS EAT PARTS OF THEMSELVES.

Komodo cannibalism

Nature's largest lizards, the 3-m (10-ft) long Komodo dragons of Indonesia are at the top of their food chain. While they usually feast on any kind of meat – from animals dead or alive – if food is short, they will eat their own young. The young live in trees to avoid the adults, and also roll in dung: a smell the adults avoid.

Lion
India, Africa
Males will often kill and eat other males' cubs when they take over a pride.

Hamster
Europe, West Asia
Poor diets have led wild hamsters to eat 95 per cent of their young.

Sloth bear
India, Sri Lanka, Nepal, Bhutan
Mothers snack on any sick newborns to give them strength to raise the other healthy babies.

Praying mantis
The tropics
The female mantis bites off a male's head after, or even during, mating.

Dingo
Australia, Southeast Asia
These wild dogs will eat each other even if other sources of food are available.

Chimpanzee
West and Central Africa
These primates have been known to eat the young of other males. In an unusual case in 2017, chimps also ate their ousted leader.

Mother murderers

The black lace-weaver spider is one of the most dedicated mothers in the animal kingdom, exhausting herself by laying eggs to feed her babies. When these run out, the spiderlings' hunting instincts kick in and they eat her alive.

Meerkat
Southern Africa
One of the most murderous mammals, dominant meerkat females eat the young of others.

Australian redback spider
Australia, New Zealand, Southeast Asia
As is the case with many other spider species, females eat the males after mating.

SNAKES HAVE BEEN SEEN ACCIDENTALLY EATING THEIR OWN TAILS.

Mosquitoes
Alaska, USA, every summer
Warming temperatures mean these bloodsucking bugs emerge in larger swarms every year, and attack migrating animals such as caribou.

African land snails
Northern South America and Florida, USA, ongoing
This invasive species can carry deadly parasites.

Crickets
Oklahoma, USA, 2013
An unusually large outbreak saw crickets piling up in the streets and feeding on their own dead.

Red-billed queleas
Sub-Saharan Africa, ongoing
Superflocks of millions of queleas destroy vital crops, earning them the nickname "feathered locusts".

Baboons
Cape Town, South Africa, ongoing
Gangs of bold baboons regularly raid food from human areas, even climbing tower blocks to access homes.

Dragonflies
Argentina, 1991
Around four to six billion dragonflies were estimated to be in this massive swarm.

WHEN FLYING, STARLINGS SWARM TOGETHER IN LARGE SHAPE-SHIFTING

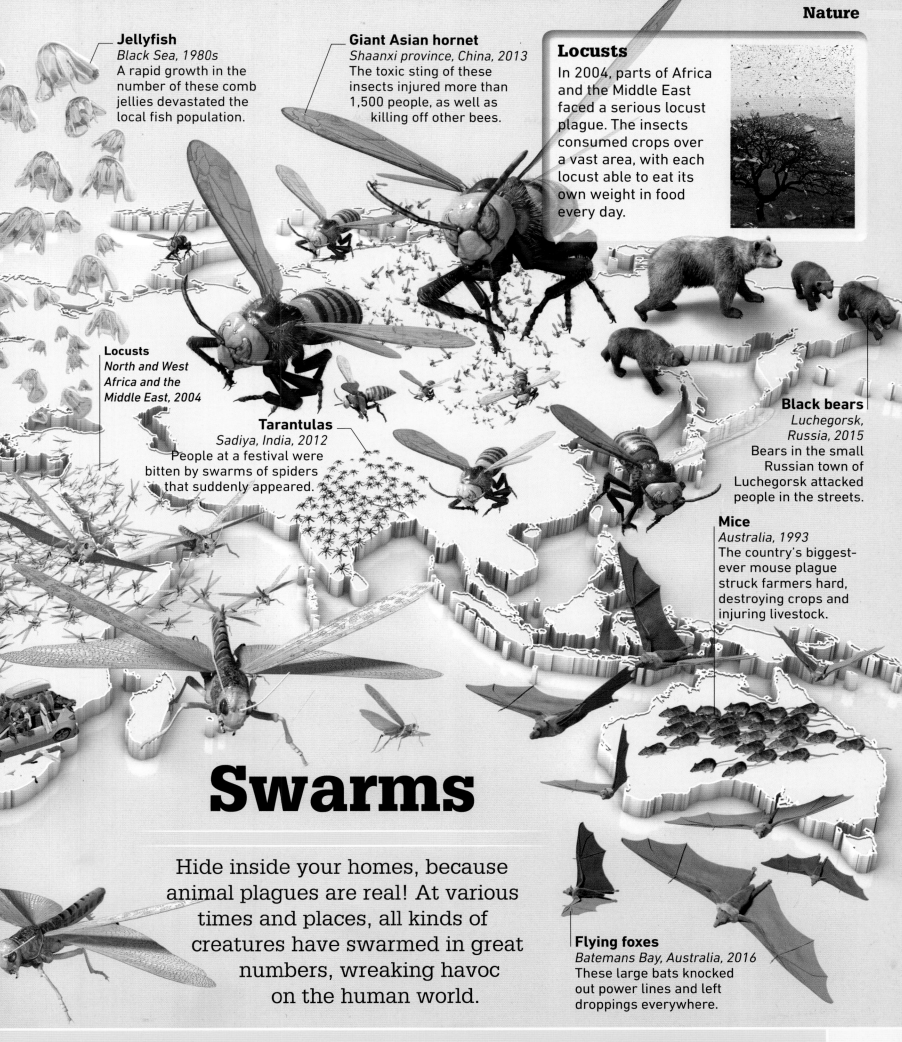

Jellyfish
Black Sea, 1980s
A rapid growth in the number of these comb jellies devastated the local fish population.

Giant Asian hornet
Shaanxi province, China, 2013
The toxic sting of these insects injured more than 1,500 people, as well as killing off other bees.

Locusts
In 2004, parts of Africa and the Middle East faced a serious locust plague. The insects consumed crops over a vast area, with each locust able to eat its own weight in food every day.

Locusts
North and West Africa and the Middle East, 2004

Tarantulas
Sadiya, India, 2012
People at a festival were bitten by swarms of spiders that suddenly appeared.

Black bears
Luchegorsk, Russia, 2015
Bears in the small Russian town of Luchegorsk attacked people in the streets.

Mice
Australia, 1993
The country's biggest-ever mouse plague struck farmers hard, destroying crops and injuring livestock.

Swarms

Hide inside your homes, because animal plagues are real! At various times and places, all kinds of creatures have swarmed in great numbers, wreaking havoc on the human world.

Flying foxes
Batemans Bay, Australia, 2016
These large bats knocked out power lines and left droppings everywhere.

CLOUDS CALLED MURMURATIONS. THESE CAN MAKE THE SKY DARK.

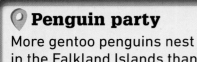

Penguin party

More gentoo penguins nest in the Falkland Islands than anywhere else on Earth. They are one of five penguin species on the islands, which host about 1 million of these birds in nesting season. The human population is less than 3,000.

Wild horses
Assateague Island, USA
This remote, windy island can be a harsh habitat, but hundreds of horses have made it their home.

Wallabies
Lambay Island, Ireland
Normally only found in Australia, these marsupials have lived on an island just off the Irish coast since they were introduced there in the 1950s.

Wild chickens
Kauai Island, Hawaii, USA
Hundreds of wild chickens can be found strutting across roads, through car parks, and in supermarkets on this Hawaiian island.

Island of the...

Humans may be the masters of most of the world, but there are some places where animals rule the roost. Many colonizing creatures have taken over a number of islands around the globe.

Pigs
Pig Beach, Exuma Cays, Bahamas
This island is uninhabited by humans but is a piggy paradise. The pigs even paddle in the ocean – much to the amusement of tourists.

Snakes
Snake Island, Brazil
Visitors are banned from this island, to prevent them being killed by the 2,000–4,000 highly venomous pit vipers that live here.

Monkeys
Cayo Santiago, off Puerto Rico
This island is favoured by researchers, who come to study the colony of around 1,000 rhesus macaques that live on its shores.

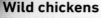

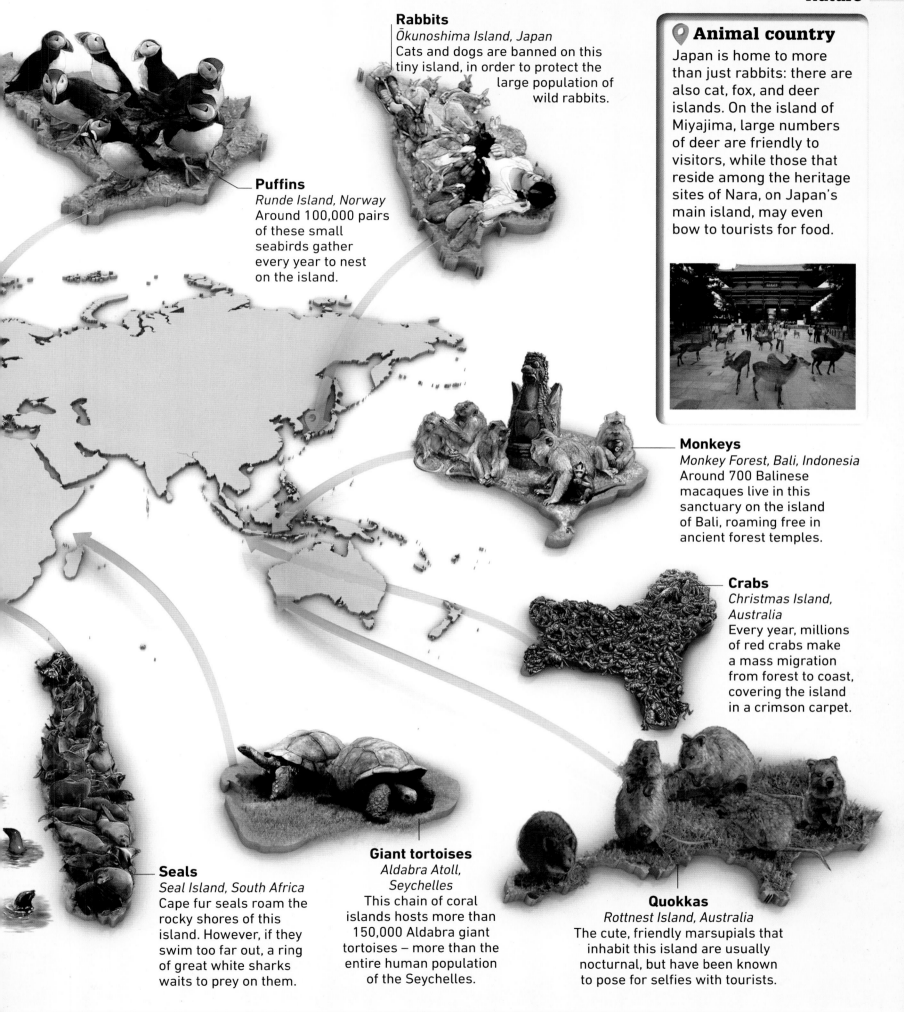

Rabbits
Ōkunoshima Island, Japan
Cats and dogs are banned on this tiny island, in order to protect the large population of wild rabbits.

Animal country
Japan is home to more than just rabbits: there are also cat, fox, and deer islands. On the island of Miyajima, large numbers of deer are friendly to visitors, while those that reside among the heritage sites of Nara, on Japan's main island, may even bow to tourists for food.

Puffins
Runde Island, Norway
Around 100,000 pairs of these small seabirds gather every year to nest on the island.

Monkeys
Monkey Forest, Bali, Indonesia
Around 700 Balinese macaques live in this sanctuary on the island of Bali, roaming free in ancient forest temples.

Crabs
Christmas Island, Australia
Every year, millions of red crabs make a mass migration from forest to coast, covering the island in a crimson carpet.

Seals
Seal Island, South Africa
Cape fur seals roam the rocky shores of this island. However, if they swim too far out, a ring of great white sharks waits to prey on them.

Giant tortoises
Aldabra Atoll, Seychelles
This chain of coral islands hosts more than 150,000 Aldabra giant tortoises – more than the entire human population of the Seychelles.

Quokkas
Rottnest Island, Australia
The cute, friendly marsupials that inhabit this island are usually nocturnal, but have been known to pose for selfies with tourists.

UP TO FIVE TIMES MORE TOXIC THAN THOSE FOUND IN NEARBY BRAZIL.

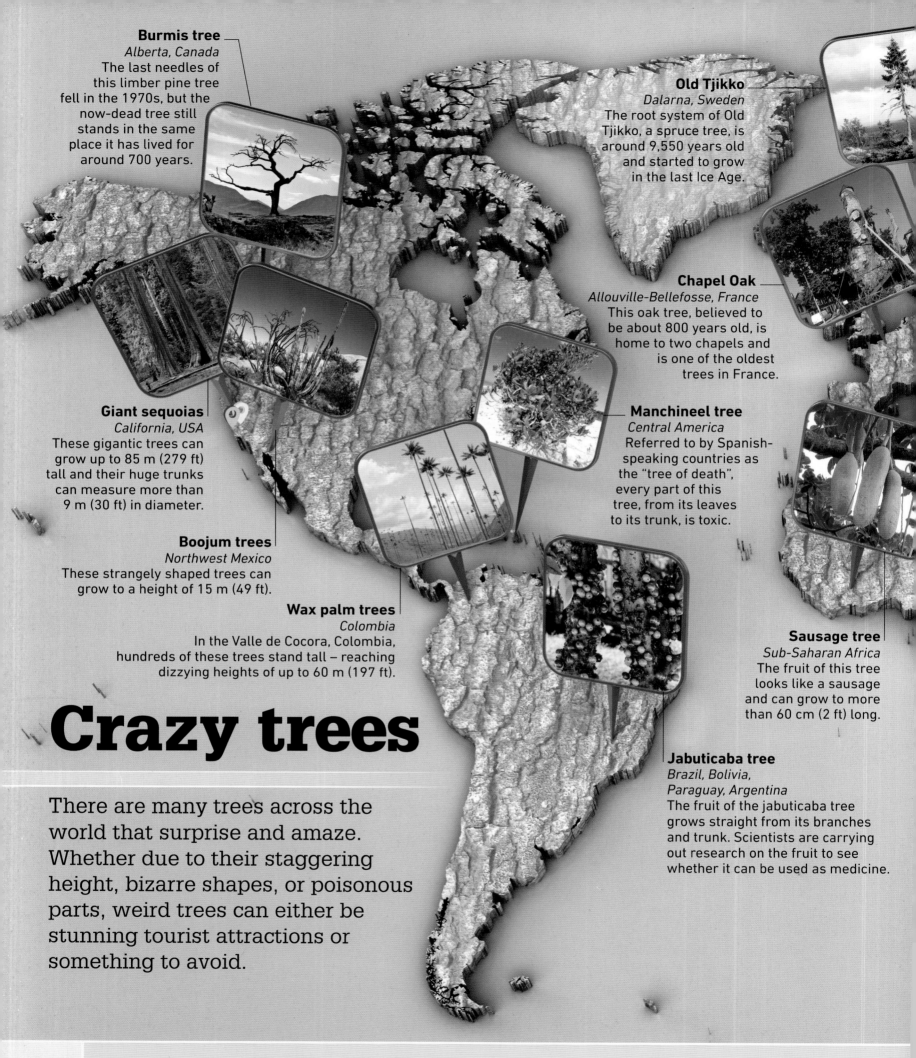

Burmis tree
Alberta, Canada
The last needles of this limber pine tree fell in the 1970s, but the now-dead tree still stands in the same place it has lived for around 700 years.

Old Tjikko
Dalarna, Sweden
The root system of Old Tjikko, a spruce tree, is around 9,550 years old and started to grow in the last Ice Age.

Chapel Oak
Allouville-Bellefosse, France
This oak tree, believed to be about 800 years old, is home to two chapels and is one of the oldest trees in France.

Giant sequoias
California, USA
These gigantic trees can grow up to 85 m (279 ft) tall and their huge trunks can measure more than 9 m (30 ft) in diameter.

Manchineel tree
Central America
Referred to by Spanish-speaking countries as the "tree of death", every part of this tree, from its leaves to its trunk, is toxic.

Boojum trees
Northwest Mexico
These strangely shaped trees can grow to a height of 15 m (49 ft).

Wax palm trees
Colombia
In the Valle de Cocora, Colombia, hundreds of these trees stand tall – reaching dizzying heights of up to 60 m (197 ft).

Sausage tree
Sub-Saharan Africa
The fruit of this tree looks like a sausage and can grow to more than 60 cm (2 ft) long.

Crazy trees

There are many trees across the world that surprise and amaze. Whether due to their staggering height, bizarre shapes, or poisonous parts, weird trees can either be stunning tourist attractions or something to avoid.

Jabuticaba tree
Brazil, Bolivia, Paraguay, Argentina
The fruit of the jabuticaba tree grows straight from its branches and trunk. Scientists are carrying out research on the fruit to see whether it can be used as medicine.

THE POISONOUS SANDBOX TREE, FOUND IN AMERICA, HAS FRUITS

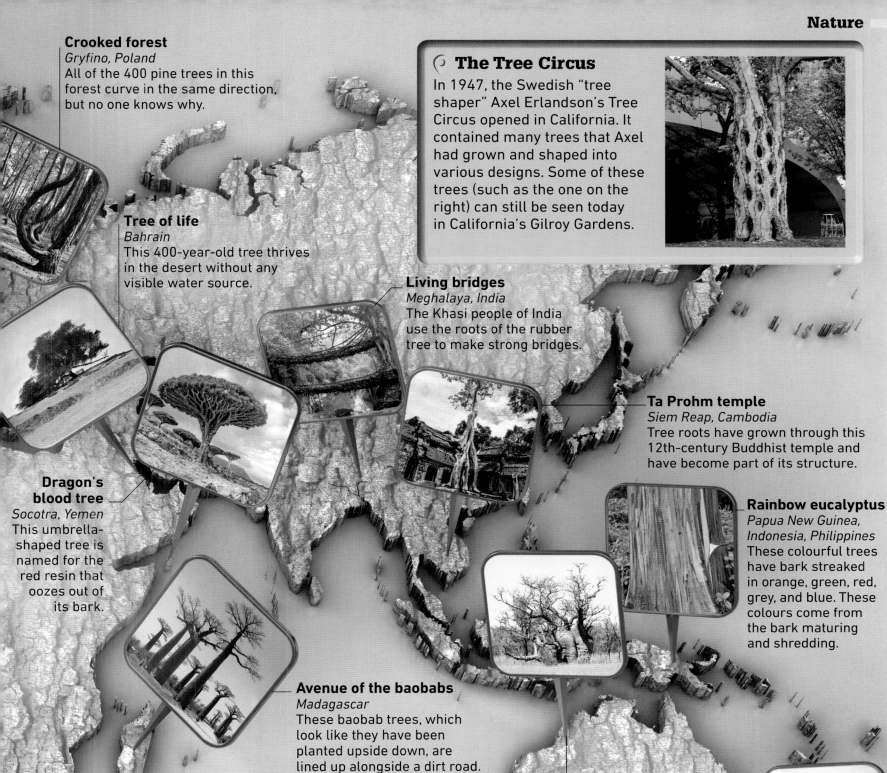

Crooked forest
Gryfino, Poland
All of the 400 pine trees in this forest curve in the same direction, but no one knows why.

Tree of life
Bahrain
This 400-year-old tree thrives in the desert without any visible water source.

The Tree Circus
In 1947, the Swedish "tree shaper" Axel Erlandson's Tree Circus opened in California. It contained many trees that Axel had grown and shaped into various designs. Some of these trees (such as the one on the right) can still be seen today in California's Gilroy Gardens.

Living bridges
Meghalaya, India
The Khasi people of India use the roots of the rubber tree to make strong bridges.

Dragon's blood tree
Socotra, Yemen
This umbrella-shaped tree is named for the red resin that oozes out of its bark.

Ta Prohm temple
Siem Reap, Cambodia
Tree roots have grown through this 12th-century Buddhist temple and have become part of its structure.

Rainbow eucalyptus
Papua New Guinea, Indonesia, Philippines
These colourful trees have bark streaked in orange, green, red, grey, and blue. These colours come from the bark maturing and shredding.

Avenue of the baobabs
Madagascar
These baobab trees, which look like they have been planted upside down, are lined up alongside a dirt road.

Tunnel tree
The giant Wawona Tree, in California's Yosemite National Park, became a famous attraction due to the tunnel that was cut through its vast trunk. When this giant sequoia fell in 1969, it was around 2,100 years old and about 71 m (233 ft) tall.

Boab tree
Kimberley, Western Australia
This tree provides food and medicine and its thick trunk can be used for shelter.

Slope Point trees
South Island, New Zealand
Strong winds from Antarctica have made the trees on Slope Point twist and contort, creating this weird view.

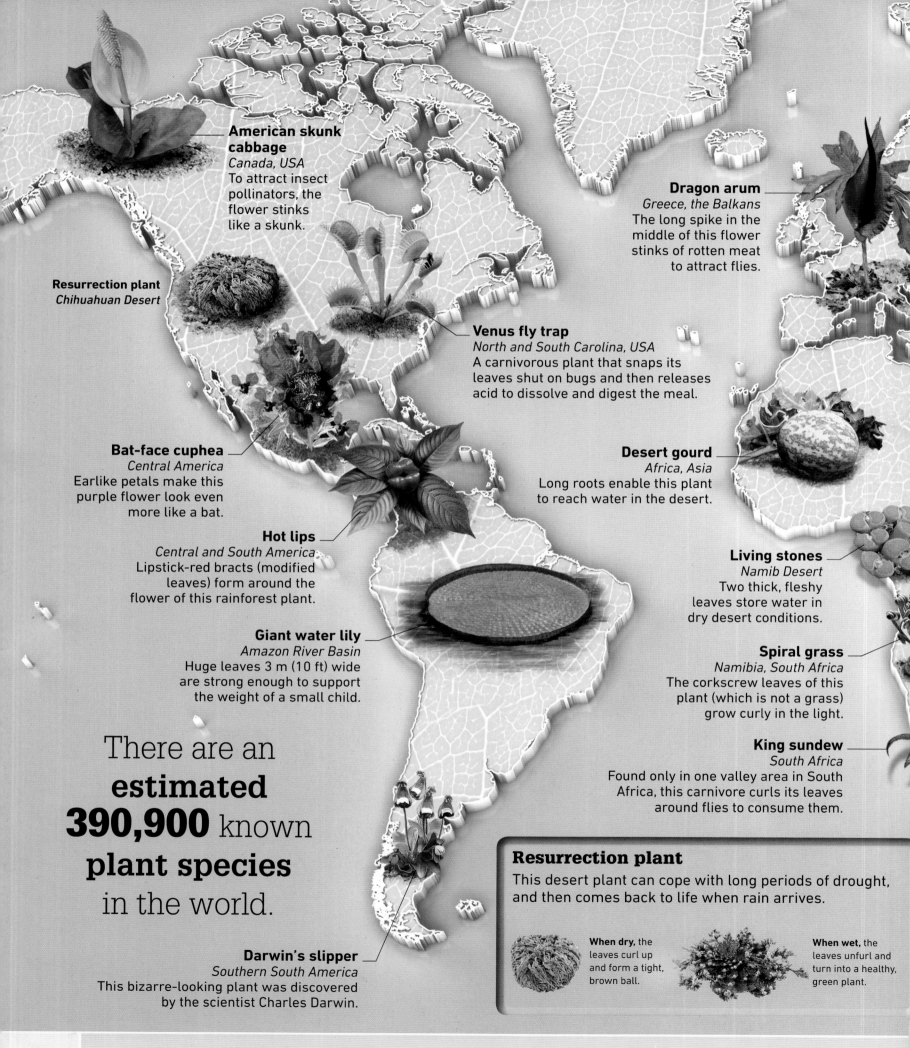

American skunk cabbage
Canada, USA
To attract insect pollinators, the flower stinks like a skunk.

Dragon arum
Greece, the Balkans
The long spike in the middle of this flower stinks of rotten meat to attract flies.

Resurrection plant
Chihuahuan Desert

Venus fly trap
North and South Carolina, USA
A carnivorous plant that snaps its leaves shut on bugs and then releases acid to dissolve and digest the meal.

Bat-face cuphea
Central America
Earlike petals make this purple flower look even more like a bat.

Desert gourd
Africa, Asia
Long roots enable this plant to reach water in the desert.

Hot lips
Central and South America
Lipstick-red bracts (modified leaves) form around the flower of this rainforest plant.

Living stones
Namib Desert
Two thick, fleshy leaves store water in dry desert conditions.

Giant water lily
Amazon River Basin
Huge leaves 3 m (10 ft) wide are strong enough to support the weight of a small child.

Spiral grass
Namibia, South Africa
The corkscrew leaves of this plant (which is not a grass) grow curly in the light.

King sundew
South Africa
Found only in one valley area in South Africa, this carnivore curls its leaves around flies to consume them.

There are an **estimated 390,900** known **plant species** in the world.

Resurrection plant
This desert plant can cope with long periods of drought, and then comes back to life when rain arrives.

When dry, the leaves curl up and form a tight, brown ball.

When wet, the leaves unfurl and turn into a healthy, green plant.

Darwin's slipper
Southern South America
This bizarre-looking plant was discovered by the scientist Charles Darwin.

Ghost plant
*Russia,
North America*
Unusually, this
all-white plant
feeds on fungi.

Black bat flower
Southeast Asia
This plant has
specialized bat-shaped
leaves and "whiskers" up
to 30 cm (12 in) long.

White egret orchid
East Asia, Russia
The delicate white
flowers of this plant
look like birds
in flight.

Masters of disguise

Many flowers come in
amazing shapes to attract
insects that will spread their
pollen. Some of the weirdest
are orchid flowers that look
just like animals.

**A flying duck
orchid's** "head"
bends down when
a fly lands on it,
bringing it in
contact with pollen.

Fragrant ceropegia
India
This extremely rare vine
grows at an altitude of
3,000 m (9,850 ft).

**Attenborough's
pitcher plant**
The Philippines
Part of this plant is
filled with fluid and is
big enough to drown rats.

Monkey orchids have a bottom "lip" that
looks like a monkey's arms, legs, and tail.

Titan arum
West Sumatra, Indonesia
This 3-m (10-ft) tall flower
not only stinks, but can also
raise its temperature to give
the impression of decay, in
order to attract insects to it.

Baseball plant *South Africa*
The fat stem of this desert
plant stores water.

Underground orchid
Western Australia
This underground plant
recieves no light and
feeds on fungi.

Sturt's desert pea
South Australia
The red petals and
black centres look
like spooky heads.

Freaky flora

These plants may not be the prettiest in the bunch,
but each one has a reason to be included in a
bouquet of weirdness. Their peculiarities usually
have a purpose: to help them survive or reproduce.

Tree nettle
New Zealand
Multiple stings from
this 3-m (10-ft) tall,
oversized nettle are
enough to kill a person.

SMALLEST PLANT. IT WOULD TAKE 5,000 OF THEM TO FILL A THIMBLE.

39

Violet coral
North and South America, Asia, Australasia, Europe
Usually found in woodland and grassland.

Geastrum britannicum
UK
This species is so rare, it has only been found in Britain.

Devil's tooth
North America, Europe, Asia
Young mushrooms "bleed" a red juice.

Violet webcap
North America, Asia, Europe
This is a strikingly purple mushroom.

Common morel
North America, Asia, Europe
Minnesota adopted this as its "state mushroom".

Latticed stinkhorn
North America, Eurasia
This incredible, holey mushroom is also known as a "red cage", because it looks just like one.

Red coral fungus
Pacific Northwest, North America
This mushroom is a delicacy in Mexico.

Strangled stinkhorn
Central and South America
The slimy brown band of spores stinks to attract bees to pollinate.

Funky fungi

Most of the "body" of a fungus is hidden from view, in most cases buried underground. What appears above ground are its fruiting bodies, or mushrooms. The vast array of shapes, sizes, and colours couldn't look more different to the mushrooms found in supermarkets.

Eyelash cup
Worldwide
The round, red cups of this mushroom are edged with hairs.

Spreading spores
To be able to reproduce, a mushroom must spread its spores. This is done by animals eating them or by the wind carrying them. Puffballs use another means: they explode to increase the distance their spores travel.

THE WORLD'S BIGGEST LIVING THING IS A FUNGUS THAT COVERS 9.6 SQ KM

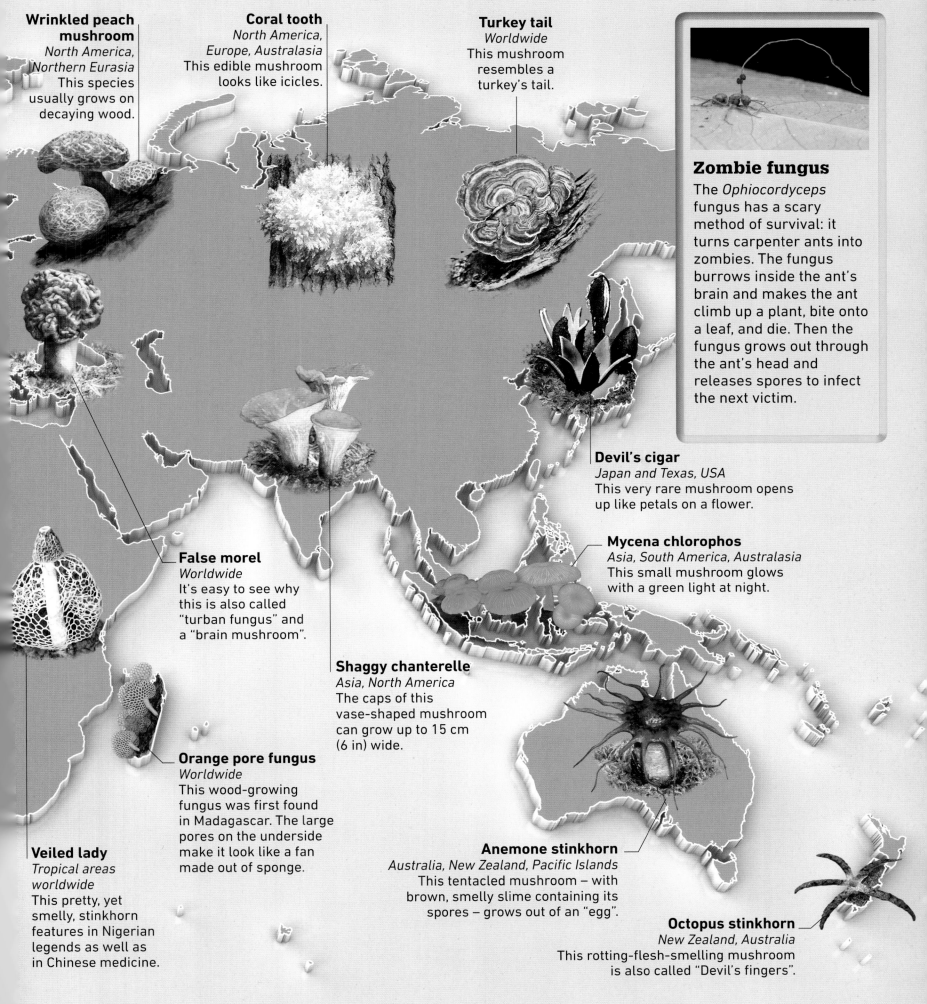

Wrinkled peach mushroom
North America, Northern Eurasia
This species usually grows on decaying wood.

Coral tooth
North America, Europe, Australasia
This edible mushroom looks like icicles.

Turkey tail
Worldwide
This mushroom resembles a turkey's tail.

Zombie fungus
The *Ophiocordyceps* fungus has a scary method of survival: it turns carpenter ants into zombies. The fungus burrows inside the ant's brain and makes the ant climb up a plant, bite onto a leaf, and die. Then the fungus grows out through the ant's head and releases spores to infect the next victim.

Devil's cigar
Japan and Texas, USA
This very rare mushroom opens up like petals on a flower.

Mycena chlorophos
Asia, South America, Australasia
This small mushroom glows with a green light at night.

False morel
Worldwide
It's easy to see why this is also called "turban fungus" and a "brain mushroom".

Shaggy chanterelle
Asia, North America
The caps of this vase-shaped mushroom can grow up to 15 cm (6 in) wide.

Orange pore fungus
Worldwide
This wood-growing fungus was first found in Madagascar. The large pores on the underside make it look like a fan made out of sponge.

Veiled lady
Tropical areas worldwide
This pretty, yet smelly, stinkhorn features in Nigerian legends as well as in Chinese medicine.

Anemone stinkhorn
Australia, New Zealand, Pacific Islands
This tentacled mushroom – with brown, smelly slime containing its spores – grows out of an "egg".

Octopus stinkhorn
New Zealand, Australia
This rotting-flesh-smelling mushroom is also called "Devil's fingers".

(3¾ SQ MILES) IN OREGON, USA. IT MAY BE UP TO 8,650 YEARS OLD.

41

Supernatural

Alien encounters
This picture was taken in 1966, when hundreds of people claimed they witnessed a UFO land at Westall High School in Australia. Fifty years later, one woman, who was 13 at the time, said, "We know what we saw."

Banff Springs Hotel
Alberta, Canada
This spooky spot has seen a lot of ghostly activity. One of its rooms has even "disappeared"!

Fort George
Canada
A ghostly phantom called "The Woman in the Mirror" has been seen in the old fort.

Mary King's Clos
Edinburgh, Scotlan
Buried undergroun since the 1800s, th street hides man ghosts.

Château de Brissac
France
This ancient castle has its own ghost – a green lady.

The Sallie House
Kansas, USA
Since the 1990s, there have been stories of this house being haunted by the ghost of a girl who died in the 1900s.

Paris Catacombs
France
Filled with bones and skulls, these underground passageways are home to many ghouls.

Povegli Islan
Venice, Ital
The bodies thousand of victims of th plague were dumpe on this island. N wonder it's haunte

Myrtles Plantation
Louisiana, USA
This may be the home of at least 12 ghosts. They appear on the staircase, in a mirror, and around the plantation.

The White House
Washington DC, USA
Visitors have spotted the ghosts of several former presidents.

Grey Man of Pawleys Island
South Carolina, USA
Anyone who sees this figure knows that a storm or hurricane is on its way.

St Augustine's Lighthouse
Florida, USA
Eerie footsteps have been heard here.

Rose Hall *Jamaica*
The spirit of a woman named Annie Palmer may haunt the grounds of this plantation.

Haunted places

Beware of these spooky sites and haunted houses – you never know what you might find. A ghost hound, a headless horseman, or the apparition of a woman in white could appear around any corner. Don't venture in alone!

Tequendama Falls Hotel
Colombia
This used to be a luxury hotel overlooking the waterfall, but it fell into ruin. That's when ghosts from the old days started to appear. Now the building is a museum.

❶ Sleepy Hollow
At this spooky, often misty spot on the Hudson River, in New York, USA, there have been several sightings of a headless horseman.

② Tower of London

Spectres of the many people who were executed here, including queens and princes, haunt this ancient English castle. Among them is the headless ghost of Queen Anne Boleyn, who was beheaded here in 1536.

Forbidden City
Beijing, China
There have been sightings of a woman in white and the sounds of flute music reported from within these ancient walls.

Borgvattnet Vicarage
Sweden
An old priest's house filled with ghostly goings-on, including scary screams and floating figures.

Bhangarh Fort
Rajasthan, India
There is a story that long ago many people in the fort were killed by invaders. The ghosts you may see here are their wandering spirits.

Delhi Cantonment Road *India*
A lonely, spooky road where a ghostly lady in white has been spotted.

Aokigahara Forest
Japan This dark forest has a spooky reputation.

Himeji Castle
Japan An ancient legend says that at night a woman named Okiku haunts the castle's well.

Sai Ying Pun Community Complex *Hong Kong, China*
When this building was abandoned in the 1970s, many people said it was taken over by ghosts.

Dumas Beach
Surat, India
It is said that many ghostly spirits live on this beach, and their whispers have often been heard here.

Lawang Sewu
Java, Indonesia
Headless ghouls are among the scary spirits said to be living in this old building.

Monte Cristo Homestead *Australia*
The owners of this creepy house have found the lights on and heard footsteps when no one was there.

❸ Moosham Castle

In the 1800s, deer and cattle were found dead near this castle in Austria. People who lived in the castle were found guilty of killing the animals – while in the form of werewolves!

Castle of Good Hope
Cape Peninsula, South Africa Apparitions of a tall man on the battlements and a large black hound have appeared at the castle.

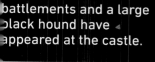

Sydney Quarantine Station
Australia In the 1800s anyone who arrived with a deadly disease was held here until they got better or died. The souls of the dead may still haunt this place.

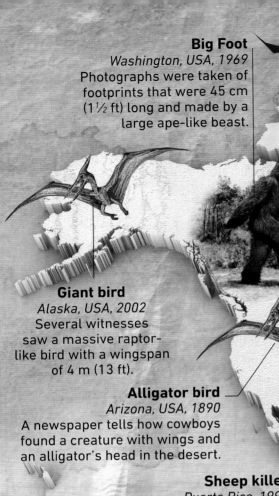

Big Foot
Washington, USA, 1969
Photographs were taken of footprints that were 45 cm (1½ ft) long and made by a large ape-like beast.

Giant octopus
Massachusetts, USA, 1817
Many sightings of a giant octopus near the port of Gloucester.

Loch Ness Monster
Scotland, 1933
Newspapers reported sighting of a large, long-necked creature in the lake.

Giant bird
Alaska, USA, 2002
Several witnesses saw a massive raptor-like bird with a wingspan of 4 m (13 ft).

Púca
Ireland, 1880
This creature takes the form of a dog or a horse and can be helpful or mischievous.

Alligator bird
Arizona, USA, 1890
A newspaper tells how cowboys found a creature with wings and an alligator's head in the desert.

Beast of Bodmin
England, 1999
When sheep were killed and a big cat spotted, the hunt began for the Beast of Bodmin Moor.

Mothman
Virginia, USA, 1966
Several sightings of a winged figure with glowing eyes near Point Pleasant.

Sheep killer
Puerto Rico, 1995
A wave of incidents where sheep were found with their blood sucked out of them.

Werewolves
France, 1521
In Poligny, three men were accused of taking on the shape of savage werewolves.

Ya-te-veo
Nicaragua, 1892
Accounts from travellers of a strange, flesh-eating vine called *ya-te-veo*, which means "I see you".

Killer tree
Guinea, 1890s
Travellers hear tales of a strange tree that could eat a human.

Giant pond-dweller
Gabon and Congo, 1913
An expedition heard stories of an animal the size of an elephant. It had a long neck and lived in deep pools.

Chupacabra
Chile, 1990s
This blood-drinking creature, known as the chupacabra, appears in tales from Chile.

Mysterious monsters

Spooky sightings of mysterious beasts occur all around the world. Some are of creatures that sound like dinosaurs from another age, while others describe monstrous animals, much bigger and more terrifying than any we know.

KEY
Many of the creatures shown on this map are strangely similar and appear in several different places around the world. This key describes the characteristics that these beasts have in common.

 Globsters Stinky, shapeless blobs washed up on the shore.

Sea monsters
Norway, 1753
Seamen tell tales of epic battles between whales and octopuses.

Varaždin beast
Croatia, 1975
A trial heard about a terrifying dog-like creature with blazing eyes.

Yeti
Tajikistan, 1979
Footprints made by a huge creature were found in the Himalayan foothills.

Jungle werewolf
Thailand, 1960
A hunter came across this terrifying creature that had attacked a nearby village.

Loch Ness Monster
There have been many sightings of a monster in Loch Ness, Scotland, but not all sightings were genuine: this 1934 photo was revealed to be a hoax. Some theories still claim that "Nessie" exists and that she may be an ancient marine reptile called a plesiosaur.

at-winged lizard
Zambia, 1923
Witnesses describe a fierce lizard-like bird.

Borneo's Yeti
Borneo, 1960
Stories appeared of a Yeti-like creature living in the mountains.

Man-eating tree
Madagascar, 1878
A letter from a traveller told a tale of a monstrous tree that consumed a young woman.

Monster of the deep
South Africa, 1922
Newspapers reported an unidentified monster of the deep washed up on Margate beach.

Hobart globster
Tasmania, 1960
A giant, fleshy blob was flung from the sea onto the coast.

Sea serpent
South Africa, 1848
Sailors made a drawing of a sea serpent 20 m (65½ ft) long spotted off the Cape of Good Hope.

Chupacabras Vampire animals, also known as goatsuckers.

Werewolves Humans who have turned into wild howling wolves.

Man-eating trees Trees that trap human prey in spiky branches.

Big cats Large cat-like creatures the same size as a wolf or a deer.

Yeti A hulking, hairy, human-like beast that lives in the mountains.

Giant octopuses Huge sea creatures with many tentacles.

Black Dog/Sprite/Púca Strange dog-like beasts with glowing eyes.

Flying reptiles Terrifying winged monsters with massive beaks.

Sea serpents Gigantic snake-like monsters of the deep.

UFO sightings

Strange lights and weird crafts have been spotted in skies all over the world. No one can quite explain what these things are. Sometimes people have said they have been abducted by curious creatures who seem to have come from another world.

Alaska, 1986 *USA*
A Japan Airlines flight was followed by two craft.

Mount Rainier, 1947
Washington, USA Kenneth Arnold claimed he had seen flying saucers.

Falcon Lake, 1967 *Canada*

Great Falls, 1950 *Montana, USA*

Vashon Island, 1968 *Washington, USA*

Cisco Grove, 1964 *California, USA*

Santa Catalina Island, 1966 *California, USA*
Grainy footage of a UFO was captured.

Socorro, 1964 *New Mexico, USA*

New Hampshire, 1961 *USA*

Massachusetts, 1967 *USA*

Norfolk, 1952 *Virginia, USA*

Prince Edward Island, 2014 *Canada*

Shag Harbour, 1967 *Canada*
A large, bright object crashed into the harbour.

Roswell, 1947 *New Mexico, USA*
Famous recorded sighting of a UFO that crashed on a ranch near Roswell.

Gulf of Mexico, 1952

Lubbock, 1951 *Texas, USA*
Report of lights in a V-shaped formation, which became known as the "Lubbock Lights".

Greifswald, 199
German

Ans, 1990 *Belgium*
Several witnesses reported a wave of silent, triangular black craft.

Rendlesham Forest, 1980 *UK*
Very bright lights were seen moving through trees and a craft appeared to land.

Cussac, 1967 *Auvergne, France*

Granada, 1957 *Spain*
Fighter pilot crews saw a luminous UFO across Spain and Portugal.

Manises, 1979 *Spain*

Canary Islands, 1976 *Spain*

Colares, 1977 *Brazil*

Minas Gerais, 1957 *Brazil*
Local farmer Antônio Vilas Boas reported that he was abducted.

São Paolo, 1986 *Brazil*

Bauru, 1947 *São Paolo, Brazil*
Report of a close encounter with three aliens who emerged from a UFO.

La Pampa, 1962 *Argentina*
Truck drivers came across an object that rose up in flames and split into two. Each part flew off in a different direction.

📍 Salem lights

These bright lights appeared in the sky over Salem, Massachusetts, USA, in 1952. A member of the coastguard, who was stationed nearby, was able to capture the lights in a photograph.

Four strange lights appear to shine brightly in the sky. They have been described as "flying saucers", though no one really knows what they are.

Explanations for unexplained flying objects include unusual or experimental military aircraft or natural phenomena, such as lightning, planets, or strange-shaped clouds, as well as other items in our skies, such as satellites and drones.

Military aircraft, such as the stealth bomber, are top secret and therefore may not be recognized by the public.

Natural phenomena, including the bright planets Venus or Jupiter, can sometimes be mistaken for UFOs.

Hardware, such as drones at low altitudes, and satellites and weather balloons at high altitudes, is common.

Lenticular clouds create oval "flying-saucer" shapes in the sky and may explain some sightings.

Istanbul, 2008 *Turkey*

Tehran, 1976 *Iran*

Gorakhpur, 2015 *India*

Hebei, 1942 *China*

Kanpur, 2015 *India* A schoolboy photographed a UFO.

Kolkata, 2007 *India*

Kyushi, 1948 *Japan* A pilot spotted a cigar-shaped UFO.

Dalnegorsk, 1986 *Russia* Villagers saw a red ball crash a hillside. Fragments from the crash site were analysed, and claimed to be not manmade.

Hangzhou, 2010 *China* A UFO sighting closed the airport.

Boianai mission, 195 *Papua New Guinea* Witnesses claimed to have seen a UFO and to have waved to its occupants.

Ruwa, 1994 *Zimbabwe* round aircraft with small figures beside t was seen y about 62 hildren near heir school.

Antananarivo, 1954 *Madagascar*

Westall, 1966 *Melbourne, Australia* Hundreds of people saw UFOs descend and then take off again.

Kaikura, 197 *New Zealan*

Beitbridge, 1974 *Zimbabwe* A couple claimed to have been abducted.

Fort Beaufort, 1972 *South Africa*

Belgrave, 1993 *Australia*

Drakensberg, 1954 *South Africa* A woman claimed that she had made contact with aliens.

KEY

Unidentified flying objects are often saucer-shaped, though there are reports of cigar-shaped crafts. Some sightings have also included encounters with alien beings.

UFO sightings

Sightings or encounters with aliens

ARNOLD'S SIGHTING OF NINE SHINY DISCS OVER MOUNT RAINIER IN 1947.

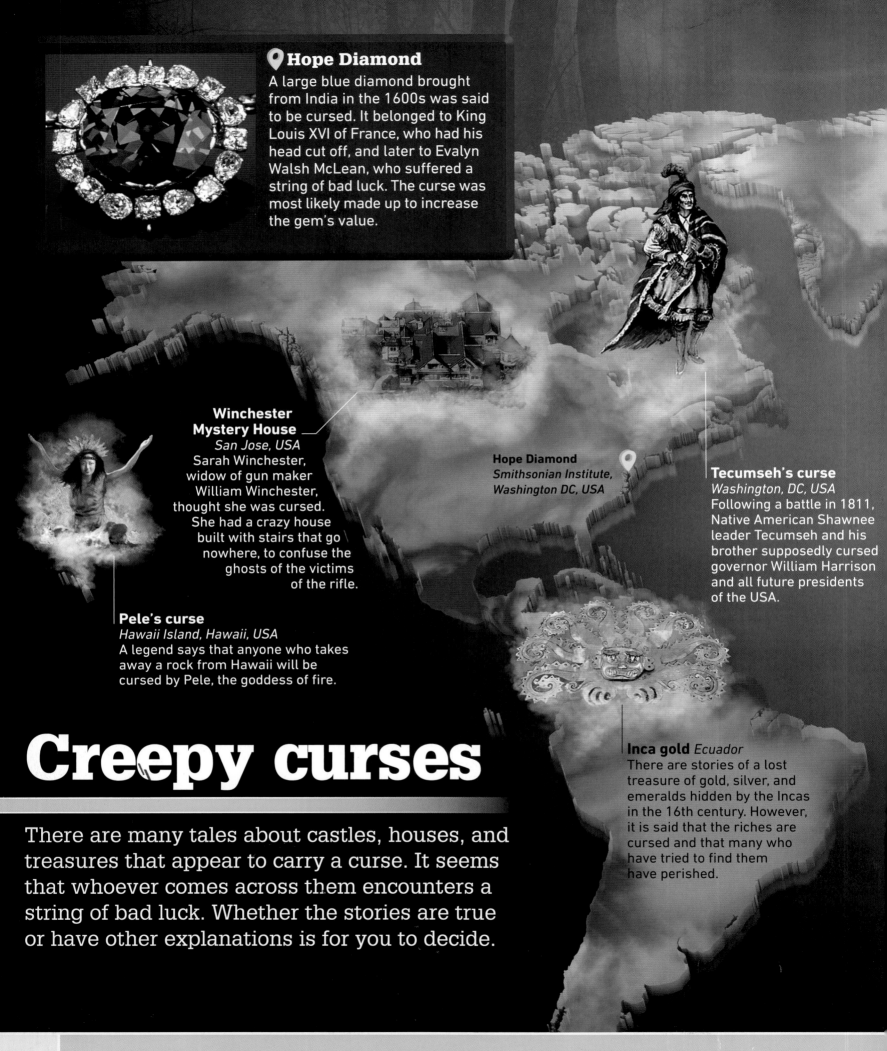

Hope Diamond

A large blue diamond brought from India in the 1600s was said to be cursed. It belonged to King Louis XVI of France, who had his head cut off, and later to Evalyn Walsh McLean, who suffered a string of bad luck. The curse was most likely made up to increase the gem's value.

Winchester Mystery House
San Jose, USA
Sarah Winchester, widow of gun maker William Winchester, thought she was cursed. She had a crazy house built with stairs that go nowhere, to confuse the ghosts of the victims of the rifle.

Hope Diamond
Smithsonian Institute, Washington DC, USA

Tecumseh's curse
Washington, DC, USA
Following a battle in 1811, Native American Shawnee leader Tecumseh and his brother supposedly cursed governor William Harrison and all future presidents of the USA.

Pele's curse
Hawaii Island, Hawaii, USA
A legend says that anyone who takes away a rock from Hawaii will be cursed by Pele, the goddess of fire.

Inca gold *Ecuador*
There are stories of a lost treasure of gold, silver, and emeralds hidden by the Incas in the 16th century. However, it is said that the riches are cursed and that many who have tried to find them have perished.

Creepy curses

There are many tales about castles, houses, and treasures that appear to carry a curse. It seems that whoever comes across them encounters a string of bad luck. Whether the stories are true or have other explanations is for you to decide.

Cardoness Castle
Dumfries, Scotland
So many misfortunes befell the MacCullochs who lived here, it was believed that the castle must be cursed.

Rasputin *St Petersburg, Russia*
Rasputin was a mystic who befriended the ruling Romanov family. He was assassinated in 1916. Before he died he cursed the Romanovs, saying they would all be dead within two years, which they were.

Tamerlane's curse
The mighty Mongol conqueror, Tamerlane (or Timur) is said to have had a curse written inside his tomb. It threatened anyone who opened it with a terrible fate. Just after the tomb was opened in 1941, Nazi Germany invaded Uzbekistan.

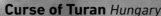

Curse of Turan *Hungary*
A run of bad luck for Hungary began when a shaman (holy man) named Turan cursed the country in 1000 CE.

Tamerlane's tomb
Samarkand, Uzbekistan

Bocca della Verità
Rome, Italy

A giant marble mask of a sea god has a curse, which says that if you place your hand in the "mouth of truth" and you have told a lie, your hand will be bitten off!

Tutankhamun's tomb
Valley of the Kings, Egypt
It was said that anyone who opened the tomb of a pharaoh would die. When Tutankhamun's tomb was opened in 1922, many mysterious deaths ensued.

Karni Mata (Rat Temple)
Bikaner, India
The rats at this temple are sacred. Anyone who hurts one will be cursed and must donate a rat made of silver to the temple.

The Great Zimbabwe
Zimbabwe
This city, built during the 11th century, became ruined and forgotten. Explorers who tried to find it were said to have encountered a curse, which was meant to keep them away.

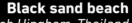

Black sand beach
Koh Hingham, Thailand
If anyone takes a stone from this beach, they will be cursed by the Thai god of Tarutao.

The giant **Bocca della Verità** or Mouth of Truth was probably originally a **Roman drain cover.**

KEY
This map shows some of the ships and planes that have gone missing in the Bermuda Triangle in the past 200 years. Even two lighthouse keepers were lost.

Ship **Plane** **Lighthouse** ● **Capital city** ○ **Major city**

Charleston

Savannah

USA

FLORIDA

Piper PA-46-310P
This small plane went down during a thunderstorm over the Bahamas in 2007.

Piper PA-23
In 2005, this private plane flew into bad weather and was never seen again.

ERCoupe F01
In 1965, the pilot and passenger were lost en route to the Bahamas.

Douglas Skymaster C54G-1-DO
This plane crashed into the ocean when it encountered bad weather in July 1947.

BSAA Star Ariel
Heading for Kingston Jamaica, from Bermu in 1949, the Star Arie disappeared over the ocean.

SS Cotopaxi
The cargo ship radioed a distress call en route from Charleston to Havana, in 1925, saying that she was taking on water. Then she disappeared.

Miami

USS Wild Cat
In 1824, this ship was lost in a gale between Cuba and Miami with 31 crew on board.

Key West

USAF C-119 Flying Boxcar
This plane was declared missing in June 1965 when it failed to arrive at its destination, Grand Turk Island.

THE BAHAMAS

Great Isaac Cay lighthouse
The two lighthouse keepers vanished during a hurricane in 1969.

MU-2B-40
A private aircraft with three passengers lost contact with air traffic control in May 2017. Wreckage of the plane was found later.

Douglas DC-3 NC16002
Travelling to Miam from San Juan, Puer Rico, in 1948, this pla was reported missin

HAVANA

CUBA

SS Marine Sulphur Queen
Loaded with tanks of molten sulphur, this ship was travelling from Beaumont, Texas, to Norfolk, Virginia, when she disappeared in 1963.

JAMAICA

KINGSTON

⦿ Into thin air
A key event in the history of the Bermuda Triangle was the loss of Flight 19 in 1945. No sign of the five US Navy planes or their crew has ever been found, adding to the area's reputation.

THE BERMUDA TRIANGLE COVERS AN AREA OF

BERMUDA

BERMUDA TRIANGLE

PBM *Mariner*
Sent on a rescue mission to find Flight 19, this flying boat also went missing in December 1945.

BSAA *Star Tiger*
The *Star Tiger* disappeared without a trace in January 1948. It was making the long flight (3,220 km/ 2,000 miles) from the Azores to Bermuda.

Carroll A. Deering
In 1921, this schooner was found mysteriously abandoned. Whether the cause was piracy, mutiny, or bad weather, no one knows.

USS *Cyclops*
A large cargo ship lost in 1918 with more than 300 people on board.

SS *Faro*
The tragic tale of the SS *Faro* ended when the freighter sank on 1 October 2015. It had sailed into a hurricane and all 33 on board lost their lives.

Flight 19
Five Avenger aircraft went missing over the Triangle on 5 December 1945. It is believed that the flight leader lost his way over the ocean.

TURKS AND CAICOS ISLANDS — Grand Turk

HAITI

DOMINICAN REPUBLIC

SANTA DOMINGO

PORT-AU-PRINCE

SAN JUAN
PUERTO RICO

Myth making

There seem to be a lot of aircraft and ships going missing, but is this area of the ocean really more dangerous than any other? Here are some reasons why the myth has grown.

This is a busy area. There is a high volume of pleasure yachts, private and commercial aircraft, and cargo ships passing through.

The ocean is very deep here and wrecks of aircraft and ships are difficult to locate and investigate thoroughly, adding to the mystery.

Hurricanes and tropical storms bring severe weather to this area every year between June and November.

Bermuda Triangle

A triangular area stretching from Miami, Florida, in the USA, out to Bermuda and down to Puerto Rico has been the site of many vanished planes and ships. What could be the cause? Are there mysterious forces at work in this part of the ocean?

APPROXIMATELY 1,300,000 SQ KM (500,000 SQ MILES).

Lincoln Tomb
Illinois, USA
This statue of the former US President's head has a shiny nose from being rubbed to bring good luck.

Blarney Stone
Cork, Ireland

Trevi Fountain
Rome, Italy
According to legend, throwing coins into the fountain will ensure the visitor will return to Rome. Any money thrown into the fountain is given to charity.

Alley of the Kiss
Guanajuato, Mexico
Standing on the third step of this alley and kissing is said to bring a couple 15 years of happiness.

Intihuatana Stone
Machu Picchu, Peru
The stone on top of this Inca site is said to give you positive energy if you touch it.

Leo Kopp statue
Bogotá, Colombia
To solve money problems, whisper in the ear of this businessman's graveside statue.

Akodessewa Fetish Market
Lomé, Togo
The world's largest voodoo market sells charms that traditional healers use to cure illnesses.

Lucky landmarks

These statues and stones are real-life lucky charms, visited by locals and tourists to ask for good fortune, good health, wealth, or love. Some of the legends about these landmarks arise from deep-held beliefs, others are just lighthearted fun.

Kissing the Blarney Stone

To kiss the Blarney Stone – and be blessed with "the gift of the gab", or fluent speech – you have to lean backwards with your head through a hole in the wall of Blarney Castle, Cork, Ireland. This is safer than being hung by your ankles over the edge, which is what used to happen!

SYDNEY'S IL PORCELLINO IS ONE OF DOZENS OF COPIES AROUND

Bridge of Love
Vrnjačka Banja, Serbia

Bridge of Love

A legend says that during World War I a Serbian soldier fell in love with a Greek woman, breaking the heart of his fiancée at home, who died of a broken heart. Other local girls sought to avoid her fate by writing their names on padlocks, clipping them to this bridge in Vrnjačka, Serbia, where the couple used to meet, and throwing the key into the river.

Weeping Column
Istanbul, Turkey
Put your thumb inside the hole in this column and if it comes out wet, your wishes will come true.

Bodhisattva Puxian statue
Mount Emei, China
Touching the behind of this life-sized, six-tusked elephant brings good luck.

Sensoji Temple
Tokyo, Japan
The smoke from the incense in this temple has healing powers. People immerse their heads in the smoke to make themselves wiser.

Laughing Buddha
Hangzhou, China
Rubbing the belly of a Buddha statue is a traditional good luck practice that began at Lingyin Temple monastery in Hangzhou, China.

Wishing Bridge
Jaffa, Israel

Feroz Shah Kotla
New Delhi, India
Believers pray and pin letters to this fort's walls to ask the djinns (supernatural beings) for help.

The Wishing Bridge

Twelve bronze plaques with the signs of the zodiac line the rails of this bridge in Jaffa, Israel. Although the bridge itself is not very old, the legend behind it is said to be ancient: touch your sign, look out to the sea, and make a wish.

Il Porcellino
Sydney, Australia
This bronze boar brings luck if you rub its (now shiny) nose and drop a coin in its fountain.

THE WORLD OF A 17TH-CENTURY STATUE FOUND IN FLORENCE, ITALY.

Pacific Northwest tree octopus
Washington, USA
A hoaxer created a website in 1998 dedicated to saving this "endangered" octopus, which he claimed lived in trees rather than in the ocean.

Cardiff giant *New York, USA*
A businessman had a huge "petrified man", more than 3 m (10 ft) tall, carved in stone. It was buried and then "discovered" in 1869.

Pierre Brassau
Gothenburg, Sweden
In 1964, paintings by an unknown artist named Pierre Brassau were exhibited at an art show in Gothenburg, Sweden. The artist turned out to be a chimpanzee!

Big Foot footprints
California, USA
A hoaxer created giant footprints using wooden models. The footprints were said to have been made by "Big Foot".

Eiffel Tower for sale
Paris, France
Conman Victor Lustig made up a story that the Eiffel Tower was for sale. He managed to persuade several people to "buy" it.

Calaveras skull
California, USA
This skull was first believed to be from a human who lived millions of years ago. It turned out to be a hoax and no more than 1,000 years old.

Morristown UFO
New Jersey, USA
The UFOs reported over Morristown in 2009 were actually made out of helium balloons and flares.

Alien autopsy
Area 51, Nevada, USA
Grainy footage released in 1995 showed doctors dissecting an alien. The film was later revealed to be fake.

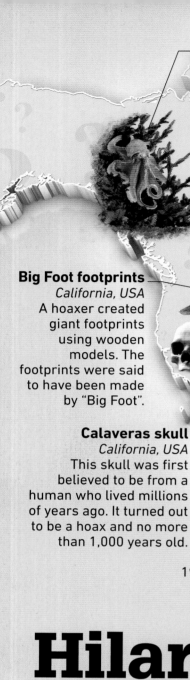

Hilarious hoaxes

Sacred idol *Brazil*
An explorer was given an ancient idol, which he was told was sacred. He believed it would lead him to a lost city, so he set off into the jungle to find it, but was never seen again.

Crop circles
Many people thought these strange patterns in fields of crops were made by UFOs. But were they?

Wiltshire, UK, was the site of many crop circles created by the first crop-circle hoaxers, Doug Bower and Dave Chorley.

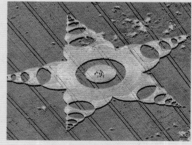

More circles appeared all over the world, such as this one in a field in Feldmoching, Germany. The designs have become more complex.

Some tall tales sound too bizarre to be true, but other times a crazy story turns out to be fact. A few of these made-up myths and jokes – many of them launched on 1 April (known in many countries as April Fool's Day) – have even tricked experts.

Patagonian giants
Patagonia, South America
In the 18th century, a rumour spread that there were giants 3.5 m (12 ft) tall in Patagonia. This was untrue, the tallest people were no more than 2 m (6⅗ ft) tall.

Cottingley fairies

Five photographs taken in 1917, in Cottingley, UK, appeared to show fairies. Many people believed they were real, but in the 1980s one of the creators admitted they were paper cutouts.

Piltdown Man

When fragments of a skull and jaw were found in 1912 in Piltdown, UK, experts thought they showed a new kind of early human. However, they turned out to be a hoax.

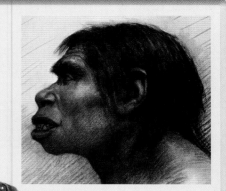

Great Wall of China demolition *China*
In 1899, four newspaper reporters made up a story saying that the Great Wall of China was to be demolished. It was printed in several newspapers.

Archaeoraptor fossil
China
A fossil that appeared to show a bird-like dinosaur with feathers caused a sensation in 1999. However, it was a fake, made from several fossils stuck together.

Spaghetti trees
Ticino, Switzerland
On 1 April 1957 (April Fool's Day), the BBC screened a spoof documentary showing people gathering spaghetti from trees!

The first reference to **practical jokes** on **April Fool's Day** (1 April) appeared way back in **1392**.

Rat fur coats
Johannesburg, South Africa
A newspaper reported that furriers were producing fur coats made from rat fur. It is worth noting that the story ran on 1 April 1980.

Drop bear
Australia
There are stories of fearsome relatives of the koala living in the forests of Australia who drop down from trees onto visitors. These are made-up tales told mainly to tourists.

ACTUALLY MADE FROM A MONKEY'S BODY SEWN ONTO A FISH'S TAIL.

The Supper at Emmaus
Rotterdam, The Netherlands
Famous forger Han van Meegeren claimed one of his forgeries was a painting by Dutch Renaissance master Johannes Vermeer. It was bought by a gallery in Rotterdam for $6 million.

Afghan hound artist *Iowa, USA*
The judges at an art competition in 1974 got a shock when they awarded first prize to an interesting wall hanging. Its creator turned out to be a six-year-old Afghan hound dog!

War of the Worlds
New York, USA

Clever Hans
Germany

Hi-Brazil
Off the coast of Ireland
According to legend, there was an island called Hi-Brazil. It was said to be hidden by mist and inhabited by magicians and fairies. Several expeditions set out to find it, but the island did not exist.

Leaning Tower of Pisa
Pisa, Italy
Construction of the Tower of Pisa began in 1173 and it started to lean in 1178. Unfortunately, the tower was erected on soft ground and when the soil shifted under its foundations, it started to tilt.

Titanic sinks
North Atlantic Ocean
When RMS *Titanic* was built it was believed to be unsinkable, so it set sail in 1912 with only 20 lifeboats for more than 2,000 passengers and crew. It hit an iceberg, sank, and more than 1,500 people died.

Columbus' voyage
Dominican Republic
Explorer Christopher Columbus set off from Spain in 1492 to find a route to India. He landed on the island of Hispaniola and accidently "found" the continent of North America instead.

Giant tortoises
Galápagos Islands
English naturalist Charles Darwin set sail from the Galápagos Islands in 1835 with giant tortoises on board his ship. However, they were not to study but to eat. Later, Darwin realized how important the creatures were to his theory of evolution.

War of the Worlds
A radio dramatization by Orson Welles of H. G. Wells' science-fiction book *The War of the Worlds* in 1938 was so realistic that some people in the US feared that a Martian invasion was actually taking place.

AFTER HITTING AN ICEBERG, IT TOOK JUST 2 HOURS

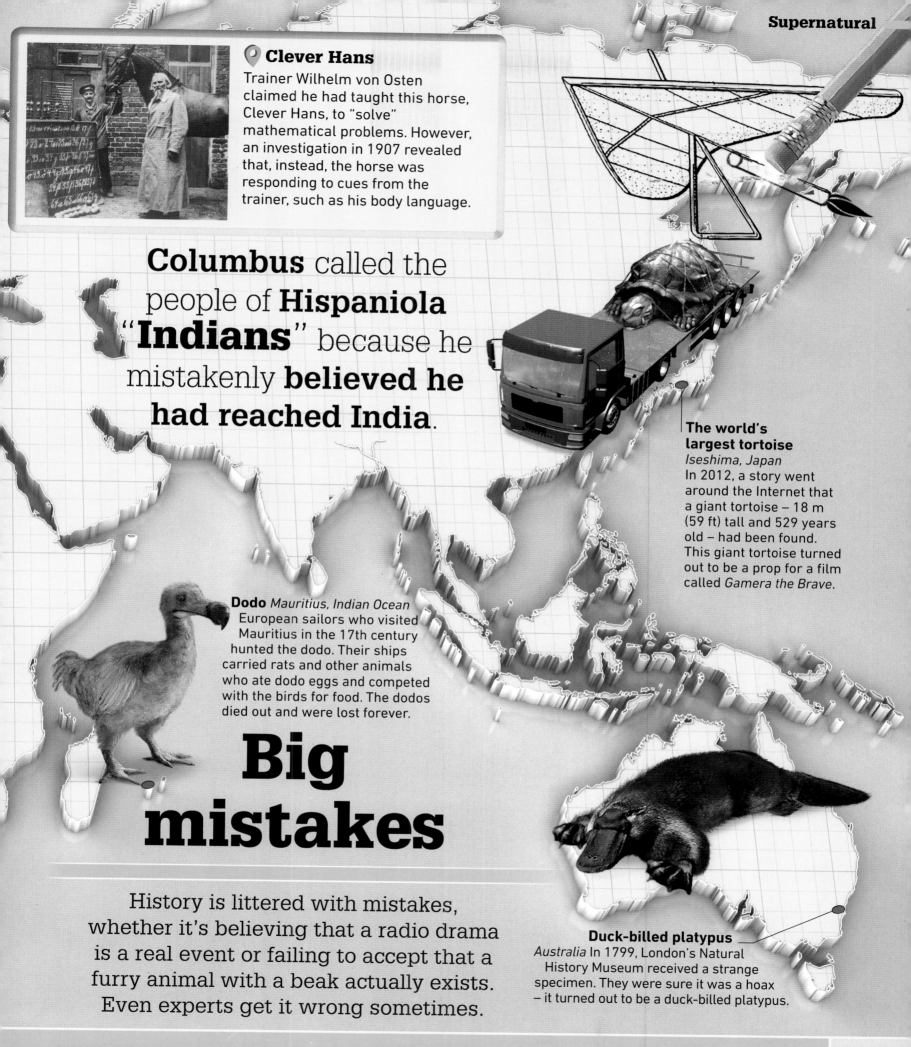

Clever Hans

Trainer Wilhelm von Osten claimed he had taught this horse, Clever Hans, to "solve" mathematical problems. However, an investigation in 1907 revealed that, instead, the horse was responding to cues from the trainer, such as his body language.

Columbus called the people of **Hispaniola** "**Indians**" because he mistakenly **believed he had reached India**.

The world's largest tortoise
Iseshima, Japan
In 2012, a story went around the Internet that a giant tortoise – 18 m (59 ft) tall and 529 years old – had been found. This giant tortoise turned out to be a prop for a film called *Gamera the Brave*.

Dodo *Mauritius, Indian Ocean*
European sailors who visited Mauritius in the 17th century hunted the dodo. Their ships carried rats and other animals who ate dodo eggs and competed with the birds for food. The dodos died out and were lost forever.

Big mistakes

History is littered with mistakes, whether it's believing that a radio drama is a real event or failing to accept that a furry animal with a beak actually exists. Even experts get it wrong sometimes.

Duck-billed platypus
Australia In 1799, London's Natural History Museum received a strange specimen. They were sure it was a hoax – it turned out to be a duck-billed platypus.

Places

Mad House

Everything in the single-storey Verrückte Haus ("Mad House") in Bispingen, Germany, is upside-down. If you take a selfie inside and turn it round 180 degrees, it will look like you're walking on the ceiling!

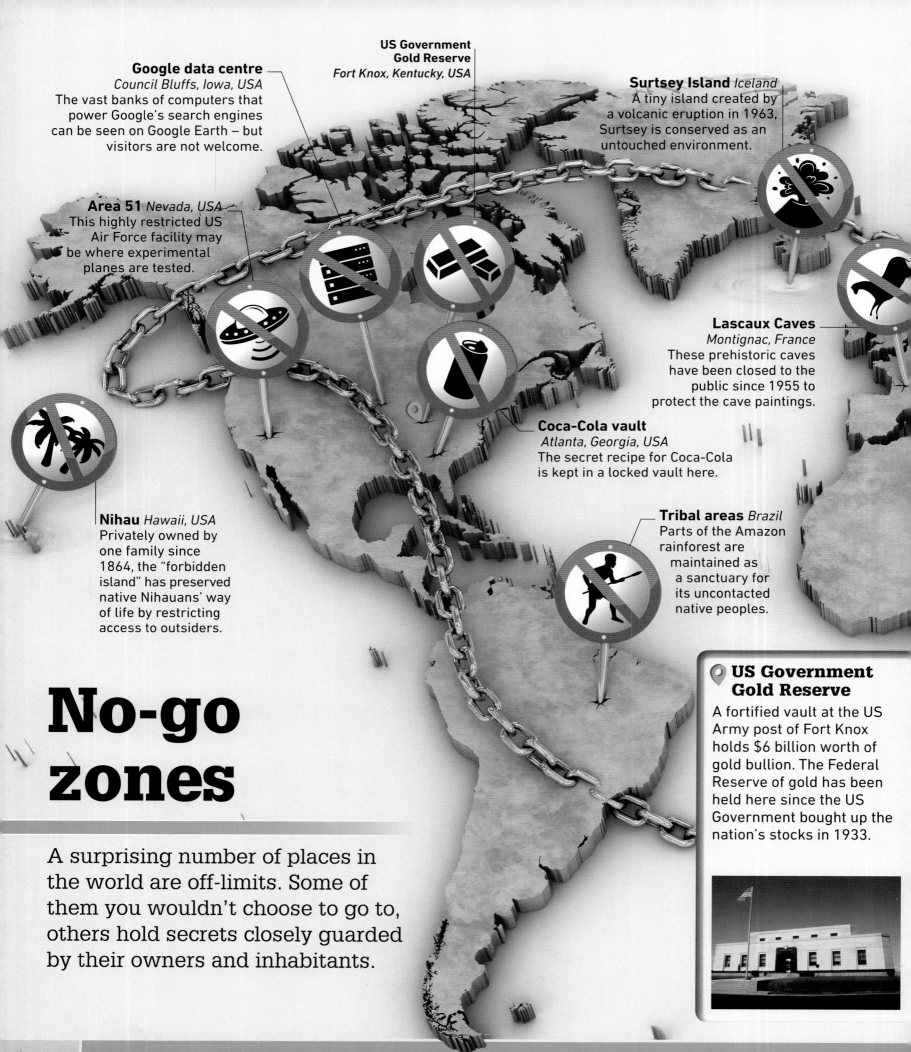

Google data centre
Council Bluffs, Iowa, USA
The vast banks of computers that power Google's search engines can be seen on Google Earth – but visitors are not welcome.

US Government Gold Reserve
Fort Knox, Kentucky, USA

Surtsey Island *Iceland*
A tiny island created by a volcanic eruption in 1963, Surtsey is conserved as an untouched environment.

Area 51 *Nevada, USA*
This highly restricted US Air Force facility may be where experimental planes are tested.

Lascaux Caves
Montignac, France
These prehistoric caves have been closed to the public since 1955 to protect the cave paintings.

Coca-Cola vault
Atlanta, Georgia, USA
The secret recipe for Coca-Cola is kept in a locked vault here.

Nihau *Hawaii, USA*
Privately owned by one family since 1864, the "forbidden island" has preserved native Nihauans' way of life by restricting access to outsiders.

Tribal areas *Brazil*
Parts of the Amazon rainforest are maintained as a sanctuary for its uncontacted native peoples.

No-go zones

A surprising number of places in the world are off-limits. Some of them you wouldn't choose to go to, others hold secrets closely guarded by their owners and inhabitants.

⦿ US Government Gold Reserve

A fortified vault at the US Army post of Fort Knox holds $6 billion worth of gold bullion. The Federal Reserve of gold has been held here since the US Government bought up the nation's stocks in 1933.

Global Seed Vault
Svalbard, Norway
In a deep rock vault in the Arctic, the seeds of 4,000 plant species are saved.

Metro 2
Moscow, Russia
The Soviet regime built this parallel metro system in the Cold War as an escape route from the Kremlin.

City 40

For decades after it was built in 1946, Ozersk – the birthplace of the Soviet nuclear weapons programme – did not appear on maps. People who moved there to work on the atomic bomb were not allowed to contact their families, and outsiders are still prohibited from entering the city.

ГРЯЗНАЯ ТЕРРИТОРИЯ ПРОХОД ЗАПРЕЩЁН

City 40
Ozersk, Russia

Plague Island *Poveglia, Italy*
Located in the Venetian lagoon, this island was a plague quarantine station and later a mental hospital.

Negev Nuclear Facility *Israel*
Signs outside Israel's worst-kept secret ban trespassing on "all days of the week".

Ise Jingu *Japan*
Access is restricted to the most sacred parts of the 125 Shinto shrines, or *jinja*, around Geku and Naiku.

Skull Island
Solomon Islands
Piles of skulls may put visitors off this island, once inhabited by cannibals.

Motuo County
Tibet, China
This isolated mountain region could only be reached on foot until China built a road tunnel in 2013.

Church of Our Lady Mary of Zion
Aksum, Ethiopia
The Ark of the Covenant is screted in a chapel here and can only be seen by a guardian monk.

North Sentinel Island
Andaman Islands
The native inhabitants see off intruders with spears and bows and arrows.

Naval Support Facility
Diego Garcia
A US base on a disputed British territory, the facility is rumoured to host a prison camp.

Heard Island and McDonald Islands
Antarctica
Nobody lives on these remote, frozen, volcanic islands, but scientists do go there on research expeditions.

Pine Gap Joint Defence Facility
Alice Springs, Australia
A secretive US-Australian base here provides early warning of ballistic missile launches. Its computer room is the size of Melbourne Cricket Ground.

Top theme park

Walt Disney World's Magic Kingdom, in Florida, USA, was named the most visited theme park in 2016, with 20.4 million visitors. The park has won this title for ten consecutive years!

London, UK
Almost 20 million people visited London, the busiest city destination in Europe, and the second-busiest in the world.

France
Nearly 84.5 million people flocked to France, making it Europe's most visited country.

NORTH AMERICA

USA
Around 77.5 million tourists visited the USA, including Alaska and Hawaii, making it the most popular tourist destination in North and Central America.

Magic Kingdom
Florida, USA

EUROPE

Dominica
This Caribbean island was the least-popular country in North and Central America, with 74,000 visitors.

French Guiana
This overseas French territory was South America's least-visited destination, with 199,000 tourists.

SOUTH AMERICA

Morocco
More tourists – 10.1 million people – went to Morocco than any other African country.

Brazil
Brazil received 6.3 million tourists – more than any other South American country.

Holiday hotspots

This map shows the world's countries resized according to the number of tourists (foreign visitors) they received in 2015. The bigger the country, the more people passed through their passport control.

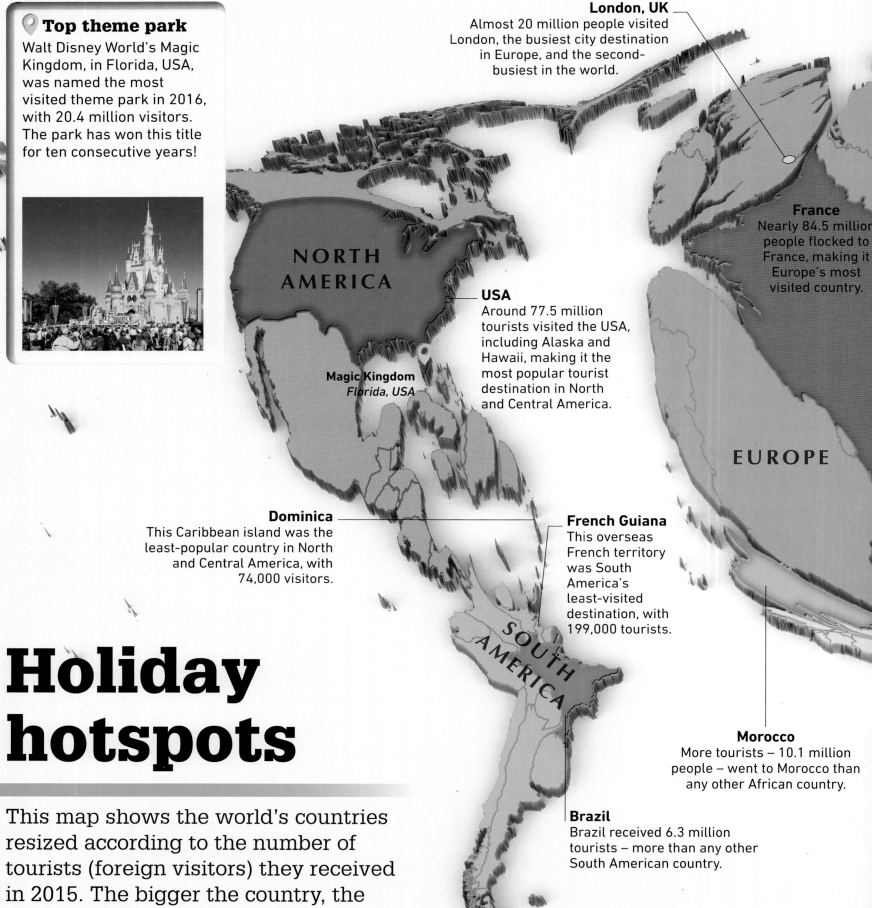

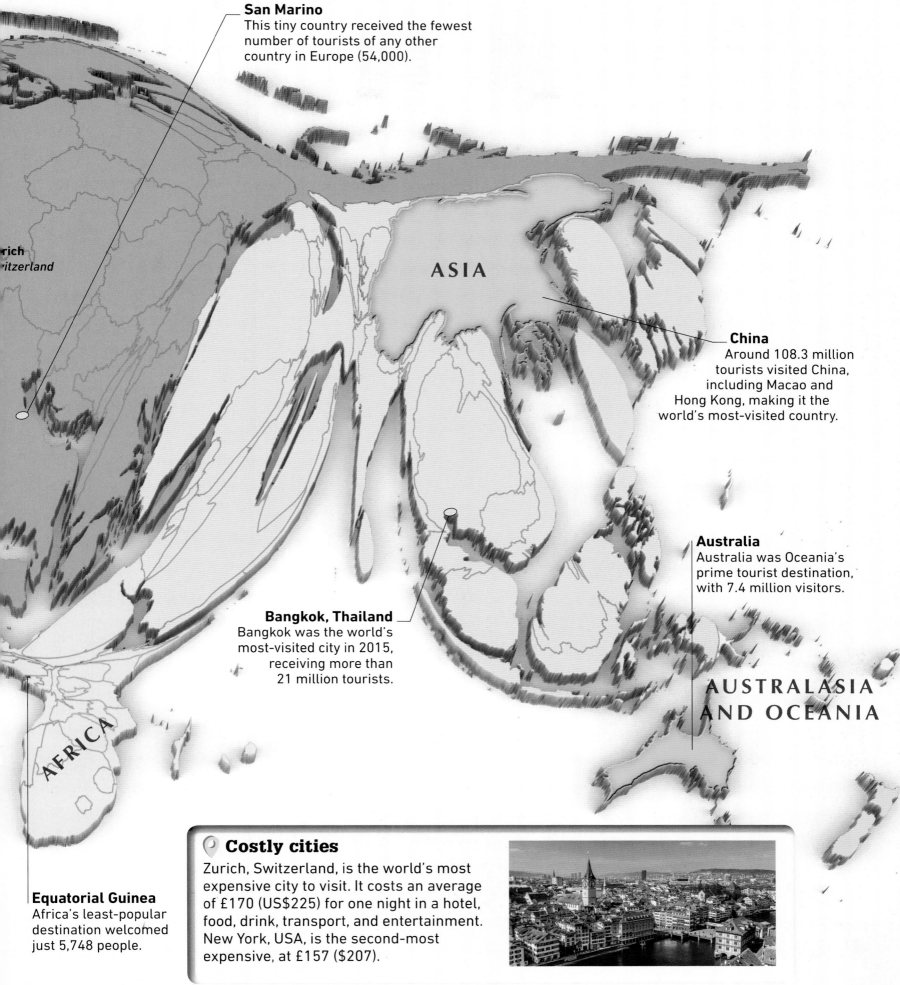

San Marino
This tiny country received the fewest number of tourists of any other country in Europe (54,000).

ASIA

rich
itzerland

China
Around 108.3 million tourists visited China, including Macao and Hong Kong, making it the world's most-visited country.

Australia
Australia was Oceania's prime tourist destination, with 7.4 million visitors.

Bangkok, Thailand
Bangkok was the world's most-visited city in 2015, receiving more than 21 million tourists.

AFRICA

AUSTRALASIA
AND OCEANIA

⚲ **Costly cities**
Zurich, Switzerland, is the world's most expensive city to visit. It costs an average of £170 (US$225) for one night in a hotel, food, drink, transport, and entertainment. New York, USA, is the second-most expensive, at £157 ($207).

Equatorial Guinea
Africa's least-popular destination welcomed just 5,748 people.

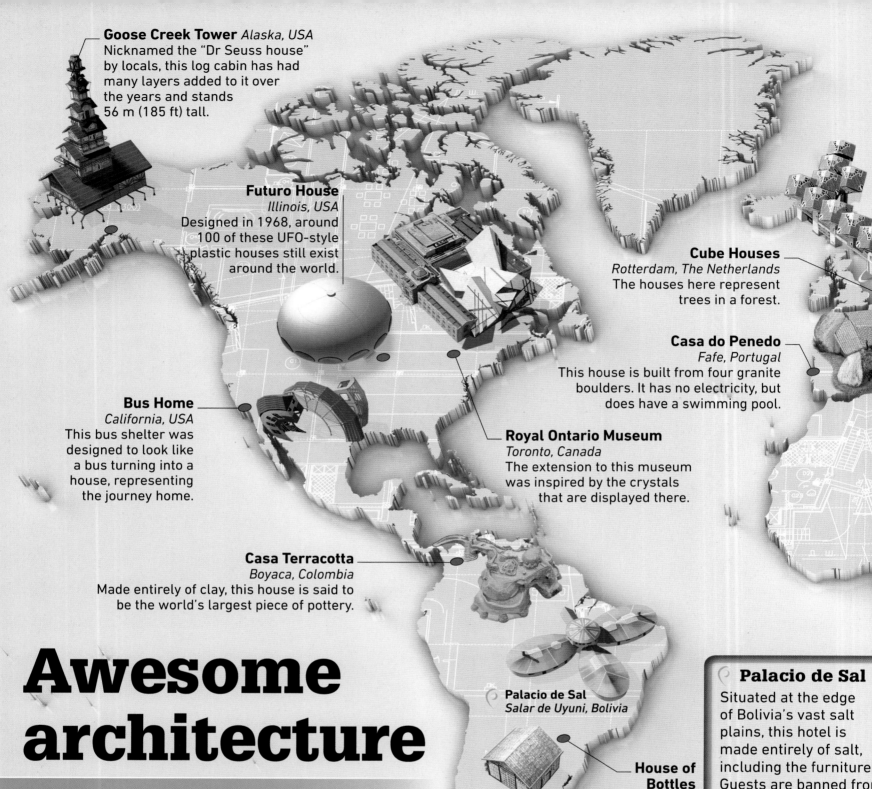

Goose Creek Tower *Alaska, USA*
Nicknamed the "Dr Seuss house" by locals, this log cabin has had many layers added to it over the years and stands 56 m (185 ft) tall.

Futuro House
Illinois, USA
Designed in 1968, around 100 of these UFO-style plastic houses still exist around the world.

Cube Houses
Rotterdam, The Netherlands
The houses here represent trees in a forest.

Casa do Penedo
Fafe, Portugal
This house is built from four granite boulders. It has no electricity, but does have a swimming pool.

Bus Home
California, USA
This bus shelter was designed to look like a bus turning into a house, representing the journey home.

Royal Ontario Museum
Toronto, Canada
The extension to this museum was inspired by the crystals that are displayed there.

Casa Terracotta
Boyaca, Colombia
Made entirely of clay, this house is said to be the world's largest piece of pottery.

Awesome architecture

Whether it's because of striking design or unusual materials, these buildings stand out from the rest in their streets. Some are in such strange locations, they don't even have a street to stand out from.

Palacio de Sal
Salar de Uyuni, Bolivia

House of Bottles
Puerto Iguazu, Argentina
The walls of this house are made out of 1,200 plastic bottles.

Hanging house
Valparaíso, Chile
This house overhangs the edge of a cliff, with a railway running below.

Palacio de Sal
Situated at the edge of Bolivia's vast salt plains, this hotel is made entirely of salt, including the furniture. Guests are banned from licking the walls.

THE INTRICATELY CARVED SAGRADA FAMILIA CATHEDRAL IN

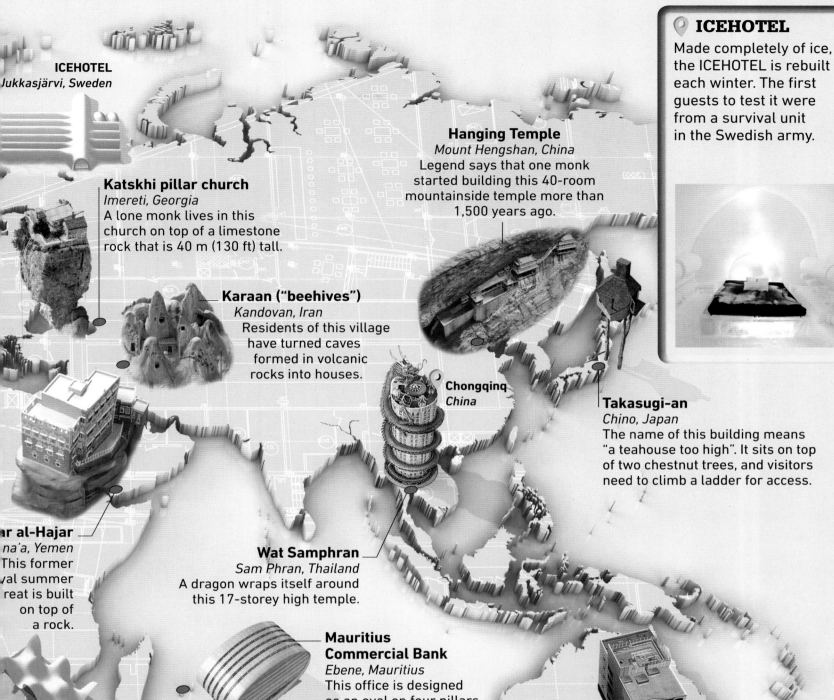

ICEHOTEL
Jukkasjärvi, Sweden

ICEHOTEL
Made completely of ice, the ICEHOTEL is rebuilt each winter. The first guests to test it were from a survival unit in the Swedish army.

Katskhi pillar church
Imereti, Georgia
A lone monk lives in this church on top of a limestone rock that is 40 m (130 ft) tall.

Hanging Temple
Mount Hengshan, China
Legend says that one monk started building this 40-room mountainside temple more than 1,500 years ago.

Karaan ("beehives")
Kandovan, Iran
Residents of this village have turned caves formed in volcanic rocks into houses.

Chongqing
China

Takasugi-an
Chino, Japan
The name of this building means "a teahouse too high". It sits on top of two chestnut trees, and visitors need to climb a ladder for access.

ar al-Hajar
na'a, Yemen
This former val summer reat is built on top of a rock.

Wat Samphran
Sam Phran, Thailand
A dragon wraps itself around this 17-storey high temple.

Mauritius Commercial Bank
Ebene, Mauritius
This office is designed as an oval on four pillars. It has won awards for its eco-friendliness.

Bosjes Chapel
Witzenberg, South Africa
The undulating roof of this church was inspired by the biblical passage "People take refuge in the shadow of Your wings".

The train now arriving on floor six...
Some people don't have far to go to catch the train to work or school! A railway passes through this 19-storey block of flats in the crowded city of Chongqing, China. There is a station on floors six to eight.

Orbis apartments
Melbourne, Australia
The front of this apartment block looks like it has large metal spheres sculpted out of it.

Tree Church
Ohaupo, New Zealand
Up to 100 people can fit inside this "living church", which is made entirely from trees.

BARCELONA, SPAIN, WAS STARTED IN 1882. IT IS STILL NOT FINISHED.

67

Dog Bark Park Inn *Idaho, USA*
The 10-m (30-ft) tall wooden beagle named Sweet Willy is actually a guesthouse with beds inside the body and the head.

Basket Building *Ohio, USA*
This was built as the headquarters of a company that made baskets and other homewares, although they have since moved offices.

Autowohnhaus
Salzburg, Austria
Despite being the shape of a car, this ecohome is energy efficient – but non-mobile.

Kansas City Central Library *Missouri, USA*
Local residents suggested which 22 giant books should feature on the library's south wall.

The Nautilus
Naucalpan de Juárez, Mexico There are no straight lines in this house at all – it spirals like a nautilus shell.

Wacky water towers
Tall water-storage towers are usually practical in design and can be a blot on the landscape. A little creativity, however, can transform them into landmarks to look out for, such as this globe in Bierbeek, Belgium.

Elephant house
Lagos, Nigeria
This residence has the world's largest land mammal on its roof.

House of Prayer
Belo Horizonte, Brazil Step inside the mouth of this concrete whale to enter a church.

Fish helicopter
Bergville, South Africa
Aged 17, Sibusiso Mbhele wanted to build a plane. Now an adult, he lives in the "fish helicopter" he made out of scrap metal from cars.

In the USA, it can take **12 years** to **qualify** as an **architect**.

Egg House *Moscow, Russia*
The design for this mansion was originally planned as a maternity hospital in another country.

The Piano House
Huainan, China
The staircase to enter the piano is inside the violin. The house is currently an office.

Dreamy Camera Cafe
Yangpyeong, South Korea
The owners of the camera-shaped cafe built it to be a space for people to achieve their dreams.

Seashell House
Tavatuy, Russia The three storeys of the house represent the sea floor, water, and sky.

Meitan Tea Museum
Guizhou, China The world's largest teapot stands 74.8 m (245 ft) tall – and has a cup, too.

Fish Building
Hyderabad, India This is the office of the government's National Fisheries Development Board.

Lutheran Church
Siófok, Hungary Angel wings around the entrance of the church give it an owlish appearance.

High Heel Church
Budai, Taiwan
The 16-m (52-ft) tall glass shoe was intended to attract women who wanted to have a Cinderella wedding at the church.

The Shoe
Mpumalanga, South Africa
This museum and gallery displays the furniture of "the old woman who lived in a shoe".

Marina Bay Sands Hotel
Singapore The ship-like "Skypark" sits 57 storeys up, on top of curved towers inspired by packs of cards.

Gereja Ayam *Magelang, Indonesia*
Designed as a dove-shaped prayer house, locals refer to this building in the middle of a forest as the "chicken church".

Bizarre buildings

Can you imagine living in a house in the shape of an animal, or working inside a basket? The architects of these structures did! Some designs advertise what's going on inside the building, but most are just for fun.

Gagudju Crocodile Holiday Inn
Jabiru, Australia
This hotel was built in honour of the 10,000 real "salties" (crocodiles) that inhabit the region's Kakadu National Park.

Glacier Skywalk
Jasper National Park, Canada
Not for the faint-hearted, this glass structure lets visitors walk out above a glacier.

Storseisunde
Eide and Averø
Norwa

Rolling bridge
London, UK
Like an armadillo, this bridge can roll out straight or curl up into a ball.

Animal bridges
Banff National Park, Canada
Animals such as coyotes, bears, and deer have their own crossings over a busy highway.

Slauerhoffbrug
Leeuwarden, The Netherlands
When boats need to pass by, a piece of the road can be lifted up into the air.

Zip-wire
Rio Negro valley, Colombia
Children take an unusual and dangerous route to school, travelling 400 m (1,300 ft) above the river and reaching speeds of 64 km/h (40 mph).

Sundial bridge
California, USA
The support tower of this bridge forms the gnomon (arm) of a giant sundial.

A bridge too far

Over the years builders have created bridges in all shapes and sizes, and at various heights. Here are some of the world's most eye-catching examples – from breath-taking feats of engineering to creaky crossings held together by rope.

Canopy walk
Kakum National Park, Ghana
A walk through the treetops on a wire-rope bridge more than 40 m (130 ft) above the ground.

Octávio Frias de Oliveira bridge
São Paolo, Brazil
The two towers supporting the bridge form a gigantic letter X over the city of São Paolo.

Laguna Garzón bridge
Maldonado department, Uruguay
Drivers are forced to slow down on this circular bridge over a lagoon.

BUILT 400 YEARS AGO, THE PONT NEUF (WHICH IS FRENCH FOR "NEW

Bridge to nowhere

When viewed from certain angles, some bridges around the world appear not to lead anywhere – it looks like drivers would drop off the bridge into thin air if they carried on. Other bridges seem so tall that cars face an impossibly steep climb just to get to the other side.

Storseisundet, Norway Approaching this bridge from the north, it looks as though the road comes to an abrupt halt in mid-air.

Eshima Ohashi bridge, Japan From this angle, this bridge looks a bit like a rollercoaster, much steeper than it really is.

Half Bridge of Hope *Kaluga, Russia*
A wooden wedge-shaped bridge that reaches out over a valley... and then stops! It is really a piece of art rather than a real bridge.

Shaharah bridge
Shaharah, Yemen
Two mountains on either side of a deep canyon have been linked by this bridge since the 1600s.

Eshima Ohashi bridge
Matsue to Sakaiminato, Japan

Tianjin eye
Tianjin, China
The Ferris wheel above the bridge takes 30 minutes to go full circle.

Banpo bridge
Seoul, South Korea
Twice a day, the bridge puts on a spectacular show, spouting jets of water in rainbow colours, accompanied by music.

Crab bridge
Christmas Island
This bridge was specially made for the red crabs that live on the island. It allows them to cross a road safely.

Lucky Knot bridge
Changsha, China
This unusual design was inspired by the Möbius strip, a mathematical shape that appears to have no start or end, and the Chinese "good luck knot", which symbolizes good fortune.

Route Nationale 5
Madagascar
This treacherous road includes some very unstable bridges. Drivers must inspect each one carefully before venturing across.

Dragon bridge
Da Nang, Vietnam
The dragon breathes fire and water every Saturday and Sunday evening.

Eternal flames

Whether started deliberately, occurring as a result of an accident, or an extraordinary natural phenomenon, there are a huge number of fires around the world that never go out. Once lit, these fires are fuelled either by coal or by natural gas.

Smoking Hills
Cape Bathurst, NWT, Canada

Eternal Flame Falls
New York, USA
Legend has it that Native Americans lit this small flame, which is in a cave behind a waterfall in Shale Creek.

Old Vulcan Mine
Colorado, USA
First ignited in an explosion in 1896, the fire in this coal mine has spread and has never been extinguished.

Centralia
Pennsylvania, USA
Ignited by burning rubbish, this coal seam has been alight since May 1962 and some think it will continue to burn for another 250 years.

Brennender Berg ("Burning Mountain")
Saarland, Germany
No one knows how this coal fire started, but it has been burning since 1688.

KEY
The colour of the flame on this map indicates how the fire was started.

🔥 Naturally occurring fire
🔥 Fire started deliberately
🔥 Unknown cause

Smoking Hills
The rocky shores and peaks of Cape Bathurst, Canada, contain large deposits of sulphur-rich lignite. This mineral, which is also known as brown coal, spontaneously ignites when it is exposed to the air.

EXPERTS THINK THAT THE FIRES AT JHARIA, INDIA, HAVE

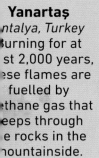

Yanartaş
ntalya, Turkey
Burning for at
st 2,000 years,
ese flames are
fuelled by
thane gas that
eeps through
e rocks in the
ountainside.

"Door to Hell"
*Derweze,
Turkmenistan*
Geologists set alight
this natural gas
crater in 1971. It
has been burning
continuously
ever since.

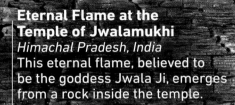

**Eternal Flame at the
Temple of Jwalamukhi**
Himachal Pradesh, India
This eternal flame, believed to
be the goddess Jwala Ji, emerges
from a rock inside the temple.

Jharia *Jharkhand, India*
The first fire in India's largest
coalfield was detected in
1916. Today, some 70 fires
are still burning.

China's coal fires
China is the world's largest
producer and consumer of
coal. It is also thought to suffer
from more coal-mine fires
than any other country on
Earth, with hundreds of fires
raging through its 4,828-km
(3,000-mile) long coal belt.

malahleni
outh Africa
ires in this
andoned coal
e have been
ging for over
100 years.

Baba Gurgur
Iraq
Set in the heart
of a large oilfield,
this flame has
been burning for
2,500 years.

Water and Fire Cave
Tainan, Taiwan
Discovered by a monk in 1701, this
flame forms as natural gas from under
the ground, bubbles up through a pool
of water, and lights spontaneously
when it reaches the surface.

Eternal flame
Mrapen, Java, Indonesia
Considered sacred in Javanese
culture, this flame is fuelled by
natural gas leaking through the
ground. It has been burning since
at least the 15th century.

Burning Mountain
Wingen, NSW, Australia
Thought to have been burning
for at least 6,000 years, this is
the world's oldest coal fire.

Murchison
Tasman, New Zealand
Lit by hunters in the 1920s,
these flames are fuelled by
natural gas seeping from
the ground through vents.

The fire on
Burning Mountain
is moving south at a rate
of **1 m** (3 ft) per year.

Grüner See

Every spring, meltwater from the nearby mountains causes everything in this Austrian park, from trees to park benches, to disappear underwater. Divers used to be able to swim freely in the resulting emerald-green lake, but this is now prohibited.

Saeftinghe
The Netherlands
Inhabited until 1584, local legend says the sea drowned this town because a fisherman refused to free a mermaid he had caught.

Old Butler
Tennessee, USA
This "town that wouldn't drown" was relocated in 1948 to drier land, but the original one lies at the bottom of Watauga Lake.

Dunwich
Suffolk, England
Coastal erosion has swept most of this important medieval town into the sea.

Kennett
California, USA
When construction of a dam began in 1935, this once-prosperous mining town was soon overwhelmed by water.

Lost villages
Ontario, Canada
A museum commemorates these nine sunken communities.

Grüner See *Austria*

Vilarinho da Furna
Portugal This tiny village had only 300 inhabitants before it was submerged under a reservoir in 1972.

Prentiss *Mississippi, USA*
Destroyed in the US Civil War, this town was washed over by the mighty Mississippi river in the 1870s.

Underwater city *Cuba*
Discovered in 2001, these stone structures in the deep water are thought to be a settlement from an early civilization.

Mediano *Spain*
The church steep in Mediano, Spain, visible, even when reservoir is full. T rest of the town w submerged in 197

Quechula *Mexico*
In periods of drought, the ruins of this village's 16th-century church rise out of the water.

Potosi *Venezuela*
After lying under the water of a reservoir for nearly 30 years, this town reappeared in 2010.

Port Royal *Jamaica*
This famous home of pirates and privateers sank beneath the waves after a series of natural disasters.

Baia *Italy*
Visitors can view this city's Roman ruins in one of the world's few underwater archaeological parks.

Submerged sites

You may have heard the legend of Atlantis, but there are also many real places that have been washed under the waves. The skeletons of these sunken structures can sometimes still be seen when the water level falls.

Canudos *Brazil*
This city was once the site of a major war, but its ruins were covered by a new reservoir.

Ancient ruins
Peru, Bolivia
The ruins of a temple thought to be around 1,500 years old lie at the bottom of Lake Titicaca.

Towering heights
Some buildings are too tall to be submerged. These towers and spires managed to escape the watery fate that befell the rest of their village when they were flooded to create reservoirs.

Epecuén *Argentina*
Salty lagoon waters swiftly eroded the buildings of this village, after it was unexpectedly flooded in 1985.

Yonaguni

This mighty underwater structure in Japan has divided experts since it was first discovered in 1986. Some believe it is a pyramid from an ancient civilization, whereas others think it is merely a natural sandstone feature.

Kalyazin *Russia*

eamana mania

Phanagoria *Russia*
Around a third of this ancient Greek city, the biggest on Russian soil, is now underwater.

Ilimsk *Russia*
Items of archaeological interest, such as the gate tower of an old wooden fort, were removed to a museum before this village was engulfed by water.

Shi Cheng
Qiandao Lake, China
Called "the Atlantis of the East", this historical city still remains incredibly well preserved.

Olous *Crete*
This was a powerful town in the 2nd–5th centuries CE, with its own king and coinage.

Dwarka
Gulf of Cambay, India
Beads, pottery, and sculptures were all found in the remains of this city.

Atlit Yam *Israel*
This submerged settlement is a staggering 9,000 years old.

Yonaguni
Japan

Thonis-Heracleion
Egypt
Giant statues, sarcophagi, and many other treasures have been recovered from the sunken ruins of this ancient trading port.

Precontinent II *Sudan*
Designed in the 1960s to be an underwater research village, the remains of this human habitat can now only be seen by divers.

t 74 m (243 ft) tall, the Kalyazin bell tower oms out of the water; the rest of this Russian llage lies beneath its surface.

The village of Geamana, Romania, was flooded to create a lake. The village's church still stands above the depths.

Adaminaby
Australia
A severe drought in 2007 exposed this town, 50 years after it disappeared under the waters of newly created Lake Eucumbene.

MADE UP BY THE PHILOSOPHER PLATO TO USE IN A MORAL FABLE.

Crazy mazes

People have been creating labyrinths and mazes for thousands of years. Their purpose has often been a mystery, but we still make them today – for the fun of getting lost.

Snæfellsnes peninsula *Iceland*

Turf mazes

Turf mazes, cut into grass, dot the landscape of England. They are linked to pagan festivals.

1 Saffron Walden The largest maze of its type in the world, this circular turf maze has 17 circuits and is 1.6 km (1 mile) long. The frequently recut chalk path is thought to be 800 years old.

Medieval mazes

In the Middle Ages, churches from North Africa to northern France laid labyrinths in their pavements.

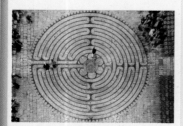

2 Chartres Cathedral Pilgrims walk the labyrinth in this French cathedral as a spiritual quest – the most devout do so on their knees.

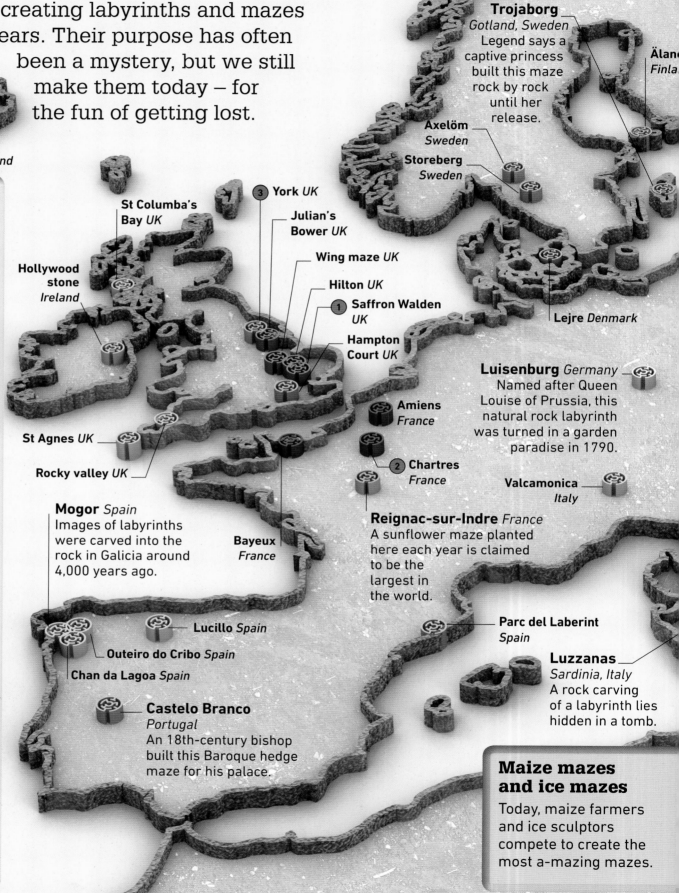

Umba *Russia*

Kandalaksha *Russia*

Trojaborg *Gotland, Sweden* Legend says a captive princess built this maze rock by rock until her release.

Åland *Finla...*

Axelöm *Sweden*

Storeberg *Sweden*

Lejre *Denmark*

3 York *UK*

Julian's Bower *UK*

Wing maze *UK*

St Columba's Bay *UK*

Hilton *UK*

1 Saffron Walden *UK*

Hampton Court *UK*

Hollywood stone *Ireland*

Luisenburg *Germany* Named after Queen Louise of Prussia, this natural rock labyrinth was turned in a garden paradise in 1790.

Amiens *France*

Valcamonica *Italy*

2 Chartres *France*

St Agnes *UK*

Rocky valley *UK*

Reignac-sur-Indre *France* A sunflower maze planted here each year is claimed to be the largest in the world.

Mogor *Spain* Images of labyrinths were carved into the rock in Galicia around 4,000 years ago.

Bayeux *France*

Parc del Laberint *Spain*

Lucillo *Spain*

Luzzanas *Sardinia, Italy* A rock carving of a labyrinth lies hidden in a tomb.

Outeiro do Cribo *Spain*

Chan da Lagoa *Spain*

Castelo Branco *Portugal* An 18th-century bishop built this Baroque hedge maze for his palace.

Maize mazes and ice mazes

Today, maize farmers and ice sculptors compete to create the most a-mazing mazes.

Ancient mazes

Tales have been told of mazes since ancient times – in fact the word "labyrinth" comes from ancient Greek.

Bolshoi Zayatsky Island
Russia

Krutoyar
Russia

⑤ Knossos In Greek myth, King Minos kept the monstrous Minotaur (half-bull, half-man) in a labyrinth. Athenian hero Theseus slayed the beast and Ariadne helped him to find a way out with a ball of string.

Mazes of the world

Great mazes aren't restricted to Europe. Here is a collection of some the rest of the world's craziest mazes.

VanDusen Garden
Vancouver, Canada

Land's End *San Francisco, USA*

Old Summer Palace
Beijing, China

① Pineapple Garden Maze
Hawaii, USA

Gedimedu Stone Maze
Tamil Nadu, India

Nazca Lines ②
Nazca, Peru

Lost Labyrinth of Hawara ③
Faiyum, Egypt

Ashcombe Hedge Maze
Victoria, Australia

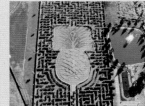

① Pineapple Garden Maze

Dole Plantation's pineapple experience boasts a maze of Hawaiian flora.

② Nazca Lines

Among these 2,000-year-old lines in the sand are labyrinth designs that may have been used as ritual paths.

③ Hawara

Ancient Greek historian Herodotus said that a labyrinth once stood here that "surpasses even the pyramids".

Zakopane ④
Poland

The **biggest hedge maze**,
Butterfly Maze, China, has a path **8 km** (5 miles) long.

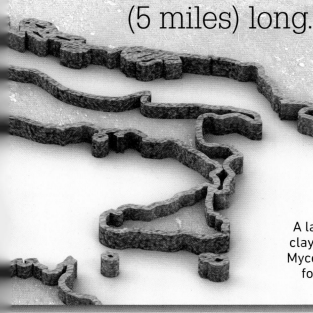

Pylos
Greece
A labyrinth etched on a clay tablet from ancient Mycenae set the pattern for mazes worldwide.

Knossos ⑤
Crete, Greece

MAZE KEY

Different maze-building traditions have emerged over the centuries around Europe.

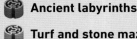

 Prehistoric labyrinth carvings

 Hedge mazes

 Ancient labyrinths

 Church mazes

 Turf mazes

 Rock mazes

 Maize or ice mazes

③ York The annual York maze in the UK has become a fixture on the maize-in-the-maze calendar. Film and TV characters often feature. In 2011, it was Harry Potter's turn.

④ Zakopane In 2016, this Polish ski resort created a new world record for the biggest-ever ice maze. The frozen labyrinth covered 2,500 sq m (27,000 sq ft).

Unreal estate

Have you ever read a book or watched a film and thought, "That place seems familiar"? Some of the most spellbinding stories take their inspiration from real-world locations.

Finn Family Moomintroll
Blidö, Sweden
An idyllic Swedish island inspired Moominvalley, the home of the lovable hippo-like creatures of the popular book series by Tove Jansson.

Frozen
Arendal, Norway
Much like Arendelle, the home of Queen Elsa, this similarly named port town has stunning sea views.

Treasure Island
Unst, Shetland Islands, UK
Britain's most northerly island is said to be the home of the treasure in Robert Louis Stevenson's book.

A Bear Called Paddington
Paddington Station, London, UK
Author Michael Bond's famous bear travelled all the way from darkest Peru to this busy London train station.

Peter Pan
Moat Brae, Dumfries, UK
This childhood haunt of author J.M. Barrie inspired many of his adventure stories.

The Pied Piper
Hamelin, Germany
Tales of this charismatic rat catcher have long been associated with this town.

The Tale of Peter Rabbit
Hill Top Farm, Cumbria, UK
Author Beatrix Potter wrote and illustrated tales based on animals around her farm.

The Hobbit
Sarehole Mill and Moseley Bog, UK
J.R.R. Tolkien's Middle Earth, occupied by elves, dwarves, and hobbits, was inspired by the places in which he grew up.

Heidi
Maienfeld, Switzerland
The enduring story of a happy young girl is set in this beautiful mountainous region.

Sleeping Beauty
Neuschwanstein Castle, Germany

Winnie the Pooh
Ashdown Forest, East Sussex, UK
The inspiration for the Hundred Acre Wood, this sleepy forest even has a bridge where you can play Pooh-sticks.

The Hunchback of Notre Dame
Notre Dame Cathedral, France
As this Paris landmark was being renovated in the 1820s, author Victor Hugo imagined his famous tale of a bell-ringer living in its tower.

Harry Potter
Livraria Lello bookshop, Porto, Portugal

Don Quixote
La Mancha, Spain
This region is the home of Don Quixote, the hero of Cervantes' comic story of a man who tries to be a knight.

KEY
These locations have inspired either fictional films or books.

Book

Film

■ Harry Potter
The amazing architecture of the Livraria Lello bookshop in Portugal is said to have inspired features of Hogwarts castle, including the magical moving stairs.

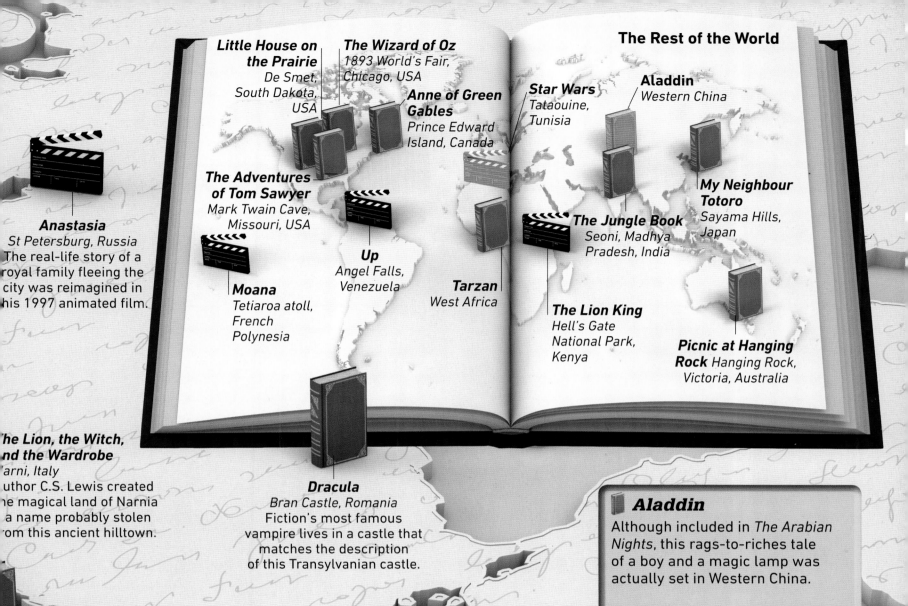

Little House on the Prairie
De Smet, South Dakota, USA

The Wizard of Oz
1893 World's Fair, Chicago, USA

Anne of Green Gables
Prince Edward Island, Canada

The Adventures of Tom Sawyer
Mark Twain Cave, Missouri, USA

Moana
Tetiaroa atoll, French Polynesia

Up
Angel Falls, Venezuela

The Rest of the World

Star Wars
Tataouine, Tunisia

Aladdin
Western China

My Neighbour Totoro
Sayama Hills, Japan

The Jungle Book
Seoni, Madhya Pradesh, India

Tarzan
West Africa

The Lion King
Hell's Gate National Park, Kenya

Picnic at Hanging Rock Hanging Rock, Victoria, Australia

Anastasia
St Petersburg, Russia
The real-life story of a royal family fleeing the city was reimagined in this 1997 animated film.

The Lion, the Witch, and the Wardrobe
Narni, Italy
Author C.S. Lewis created the magical land of Narnia — a name probably stolen from this ancient hilltown.

Dracula
Bran Castle, Romania
Fiction's most famous vampire lives in a castle that matches the description of this Transylvanian castle.

Aladdin
Although included in *The Arabian Nights*, this rags-to-riches tale of a boy and a magic lamp was actually set in Western China.

Sleeping Beauty
With its snowy-white walls and stunning scenery, Neuschwanstein Castle in Germany bears a strong resemblance to the palace in Disney's classic fairytale film.

Star Wars
Luke Skywalker's home planet Tatooine has an Earth counterpart: the town of Tataouine in Tunisia. Many scenes for the films were shot in its nearby hills and villages.

Finland
This country has 179,584 islands – more than any other country in the world.

Italy
There are three countries within Italy's borders: Italy, San Marino, and the Vatican City.

Uzbekistan
This is one of only two double-landlocked countries (a country surrounded by other countries that have no borders with oceans). The other is Liechtenstein.

Russia
About half of this vast country is covered in trees. In fact, around 20 per cent of the world's forests can be found here.

China
Despite crossing five different time zones, the whole of China operates on the same time: GMT +8 hours (the time zone of China's capital, Beijing).

Istanbul
Turkey
This is the only city in the world to be in two continents: Asia and Europe. The Bosphorus Strait runs through the city's centre, creating the continental divide.

River Niger
Guinea–Nigeria
The source of this river is only 150 km (93 miles) from the coast, but it runs 4,200 km (2,600 miles) inland before flowing into the sea in Nigeria.

Saudi Arabia
This is the largest of 18 countries in the world that have no river.

Samosir Island
Indonesia
The world's largest island-on-an-island covers 640 sq km (247 sq miles).

Vulcan Point
Luzon Island, Philippines
This is an island in a lake that is on an island in a lake on a bigger island.

⦿ Mount Chimborazo
At 8,848 m (29,029 ft), Mount Everest is the world's tallest mountain. Mount Chimborazo is 2,580 m (8,465 ft) shorter, but its summit is further away from Earth's core than Everest's. This is because Earth is not a perfect sphere, but – like a ball held tightly between two hands – is squashed at the poles, creating a bulge in the middle.

THERE ARE 300 LAKES UNDER THE ANTARCTIC ICE THAT DON'T

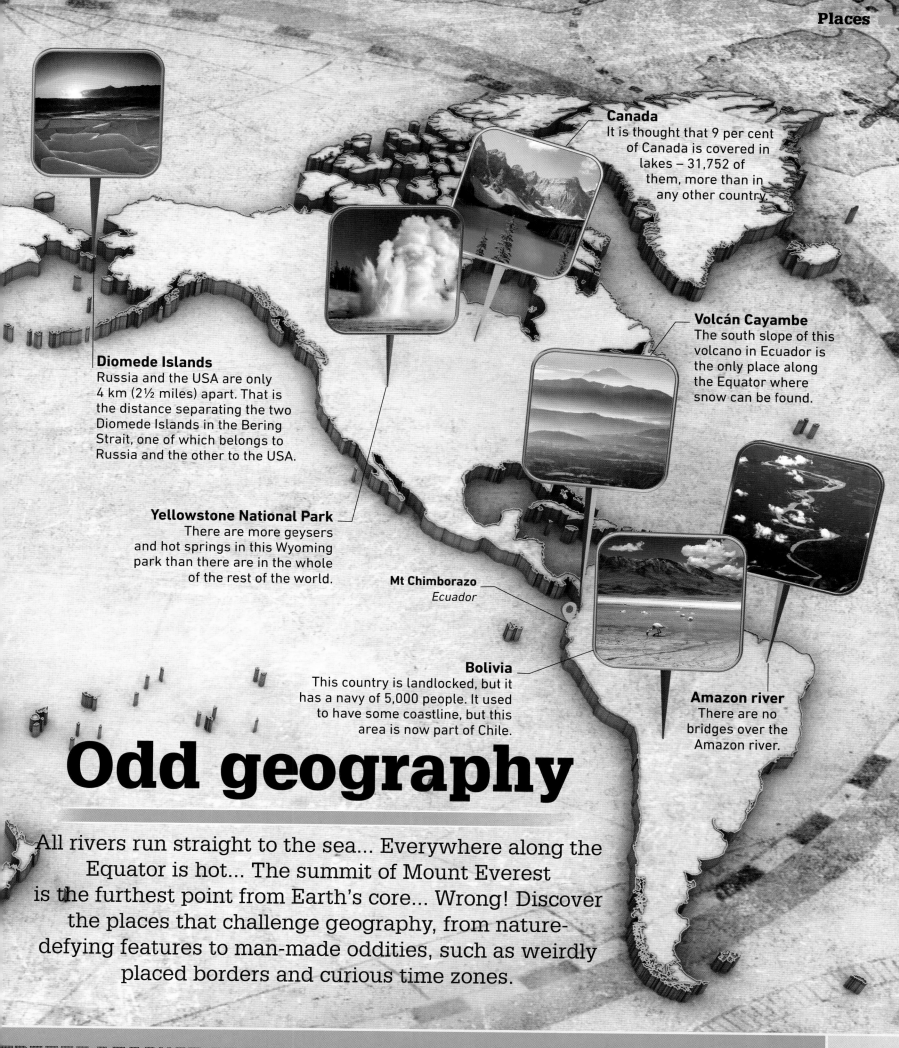

Canada
It is thought that 9 per cent of Canada is covered in lakes – 31,752 of them, more than in any other country.

Volcán Cayambe
The south slope of this volcano in Ecuador is the only place along the Equator where snow can be found.

Diomede Islands
Russia and the USA are only 4 km (2½ miles) apart. That is the distance separating the two Diomede Islands in the Bering Strait, one of which belongs to Russia and the other to the USA.

Yellowstone National Park
There are more geysers and hot springs in this Wyoming park than there are in the whole of the rest of the world.

Mt Chimborazo
Ecuador

Bolivia
This country is landlocked, but it has a navy of 5,000 people. It used to have some coastline, but this area is now part of Chile.

Amazon river
There are no bridges over the Amazon river.

Odd geography

All rivers run straight to the sea... Everywhere along the Equator is hot... The summit of Mount Everest is the furthest point from Earth's core... Wrong! Discover the places that challenge geography, from nature-defying features to man-made oddities, such as weirdly placed borders and curious time zones.

FREEZE BECAUSE OF THE WARMTH FROM EARTH'S CORE.

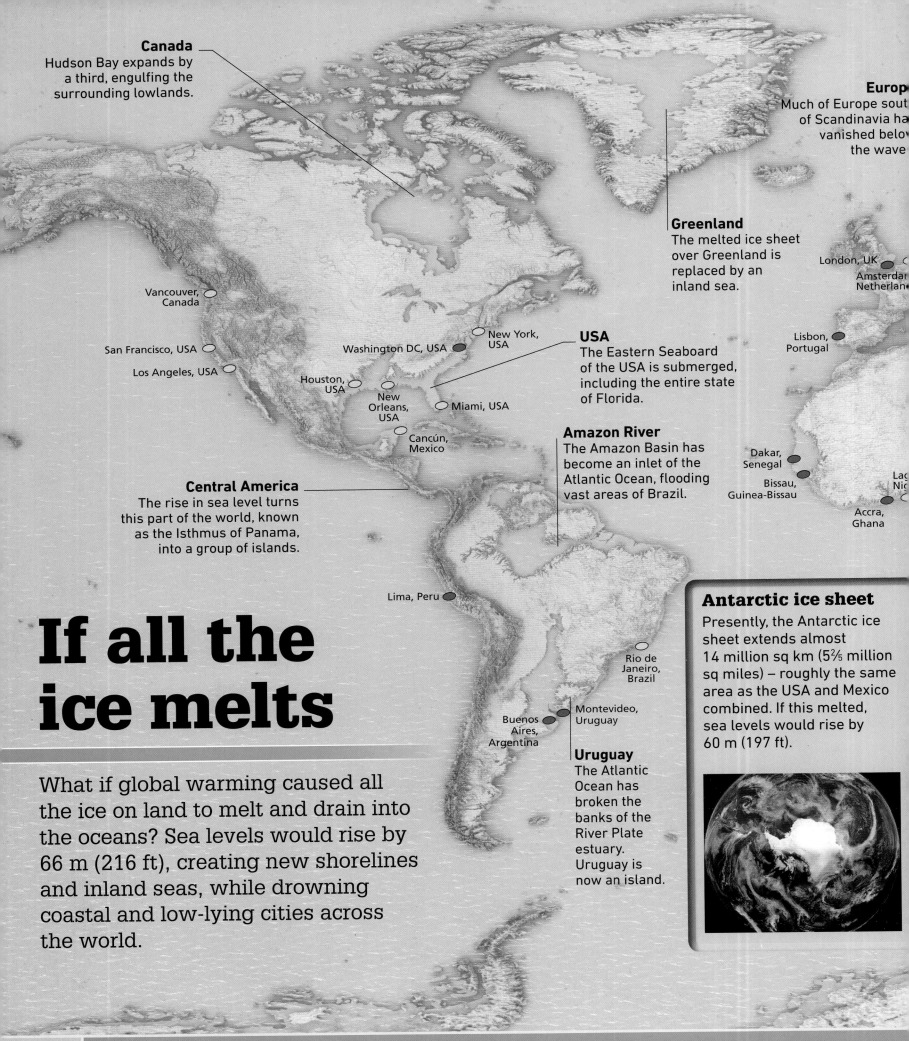

Canada
Hudson Bay expands by a third, engulfing the surrounding lowlands.

Europe
Much of Europe south of Scandinavia has vanished below the waves

Greenland
The melted ice sheet over Greenland is replaced by an inland sea.

London, UK

Amsterdam, Netherlands

Vancouver, Canada

New York, USA

USA
The Eastern Seaboard of the USA is submerged, including the entire state of Florida.

Lisbon, Portugal

San Francisco, USA

Washington DC, USA

Los Angeles, USA

Houston, USA

New Orleans, USA

Miami, USA

Cancún, Mexico

Amazon River
The Amazon Basin has become an inlet of the Atlantic Ocean, flooding vast areas of Brazil.

Dakar, Senegal

Bissau, Guinea-Bissau

Lagos, Nigeria

Accra, Ghana

Central America
The rise in sea level turns this part of the world, known as the Isthmus of Panama, into a group of islands.

Lima, Peru

If all the ice melts

Rio de Janeiro, Brazil

Antarctic ice sheet
Presently, the Antarctic ice sheet extends almost 14 million sq km ($5\frac{2}{5}$ million sq miles) – roughly the same area as the USA and Mexico combined. If this melted, sea levels would rise by 60 m (197 ft).

Montevideo, Uruguay

Buenos Aires, Argentina

Uruguay
The Atlantic Ocean has broken the banks of the River Plate estuary. Uruguay is now an island.

What if global warming caused all the ice on land to melt and drain into the oceans? Sea levels would rise by 66 m (216 ft), creating new shorelines and inland seas, while drowning coastal and low-lying cities across the world.

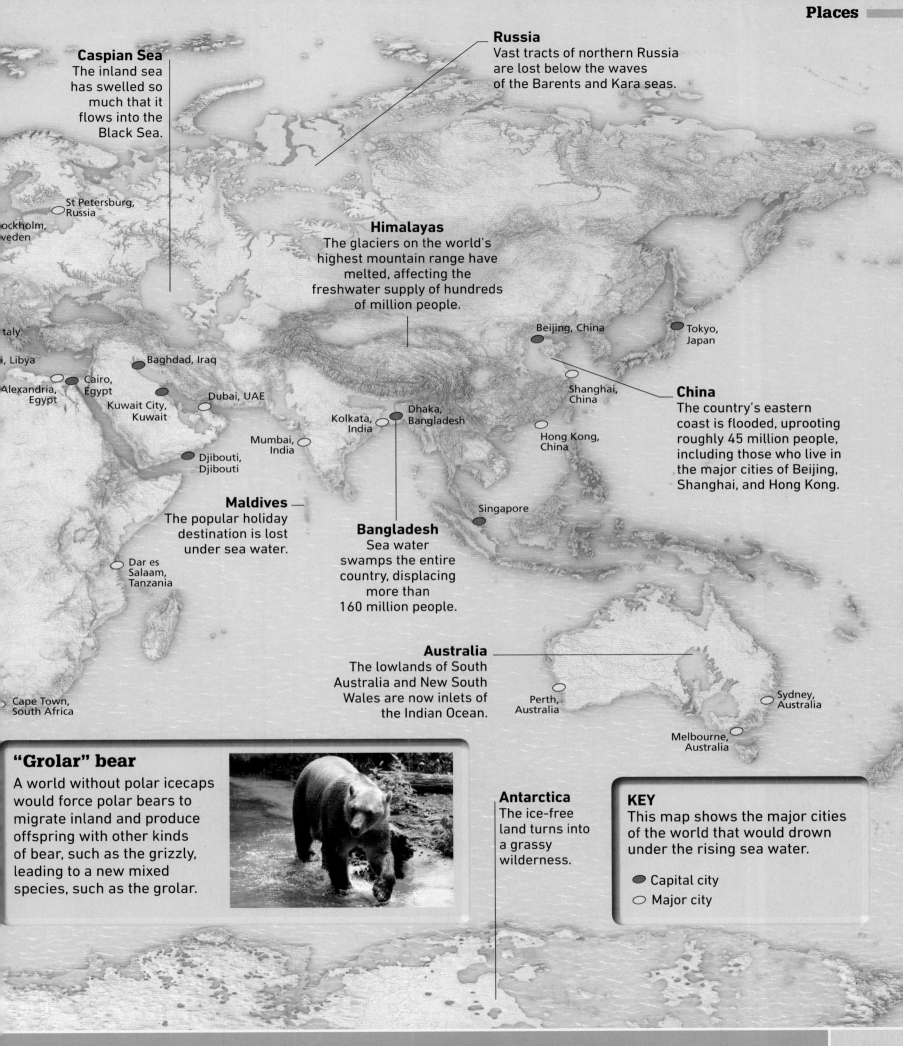

Caspian Sea
The inland sea has swelled so much that it flows into the Black Sea.

Russia
Vast tracts of northern Russia are lost below the waves of the Barents and Kara seas.

St Petersburg, Russia

ockholm, veden

Himalayas
The glaciers on the world's highest mountain range have melted, affecting the freshwater supply of hundreds of million people.

Beijing, China

Tokyo, Japan

taly

i, Libya

Baghdad, Iraq

Cairo, Egypt

Alexandria, Egypt

Kuwait City, Kuwait

Dubai, UAE

Shanghai, China

China
The country's eastern coast is flooded, uprooting roughly 45 million people, including those who live in the major cities of Beijing, Shanghai, and Hong Kong.

Kolkata, India

Dhaka, Bangladesh

Mumbai, India

Djibouti, Djibouti

Hong Kong, China

Maldives —
The popular holiday destination is lost under sea water.

Dar es Salaam, Tanzania

Singapore

Bangladesh
Sea water swamps the entire country, displacing more than 160 million people.

Australia
The lowlands of South Australia and New South Wales are now inlets of the Indian Ocean.

Perth, Australia

Sydney, Australia

Cape Town, South Africa

Melbourne, Australia

"Grolar" bear
A world without polar icecaps would force polar bears to migrate inland and produce offspring with other kinds of bear, such as the grizzly, leading to a new mixed species, such as the grolar.

Antarctica
The ice-free land turns into a grassy wilderness.

KEY
This map shows the major cities of the world that would drown under the rising sea water.

● Capital city
○ Major city

ARE MELTING AT A RATE OF NINE PER CENT EVERY DECADE.

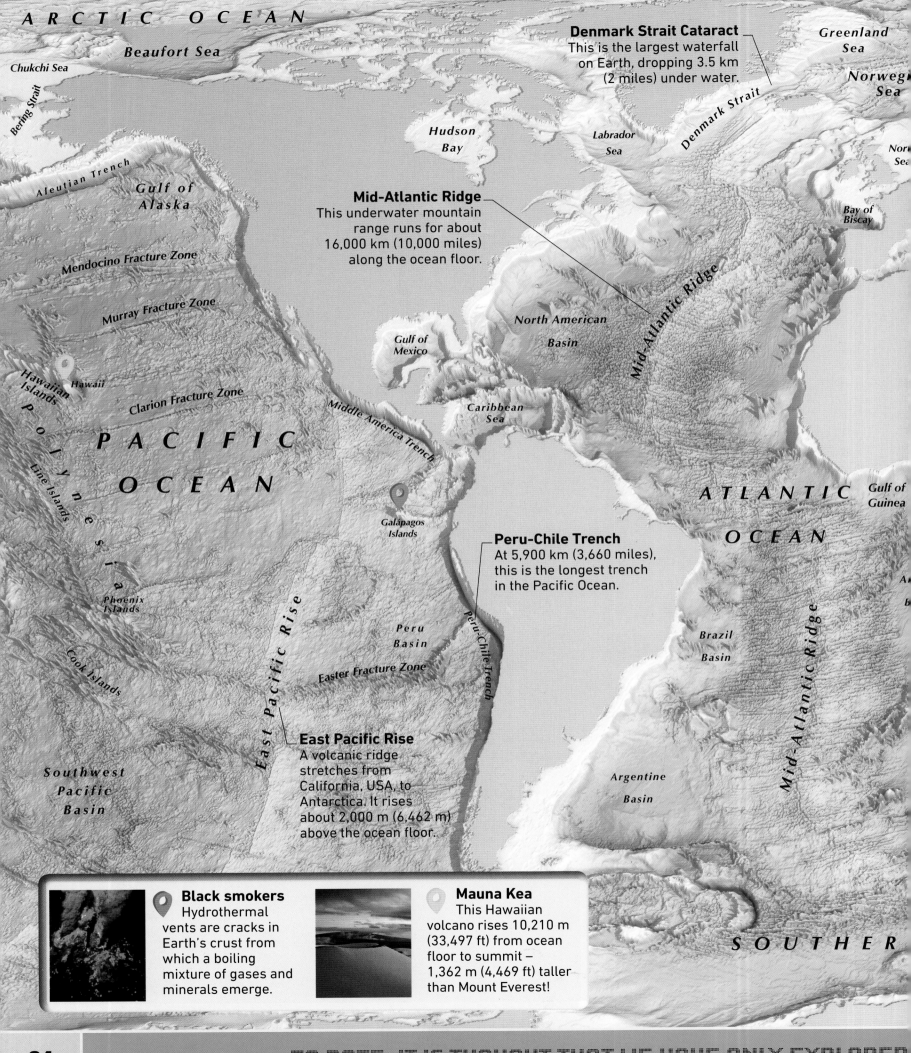

ARCTIC OCEAN

Beaufort Sea

Chukchi Sea

Bering Strait

Denmark Strait Cataract
This is the largest waterfall on Earth, dropping 3.5 km (2 miles) under water.

Greenland Sea

Norweg Sea

Hudson Bay

Labrador Sea

Denmark Strait

Nor Se

Aleutian Trench

Gulf of Alaska

Mid-Atlantic Ridge
This underwater mountain range runs for about 16,000 km (10,000 miles) along the ocean floor.

Bay of Biscay

Mendocino Fracture Zone

Murray Fracture Zone

Gulf of Mexico

North American Basin

Mid-Atlantic Ridge

Hawaiian Islands

Hawaii

Clarion Fracture Zone

Middle America Trench

Caribbean Sea

P
o
l
y
n
e
s
i
a

PACIFIC

OCEAN

ATLANTIC

OCEAN

Gulf of Guinea

Line Islands

Galápagos Islands

Peru-Chile Trench
At 5,900 km (3,660 miles), this is the longest trench in the Pacific Ocean.

Phoenix Islands

East Pacific Rise

Peru Basin

Peru-Chile Trench

Brazil Basin

Cook Islands

Easter Fracture Zone

Mid-Atlantic Ridge

Southwest Pacific Basin

East Pacific Rise
A volcanic ridge stretches from California, USA, to Antarctica. It rises about 2,000 m (6,462 m) above the ocean floor.

Argentine Basin

Black smokers
Hydrothermal vents are cracks in Earth's crust from which a boiling mixture of gases and minerals emerge.

Mauna Kea
This Hawaiian volcano rises 10,210 m (33,497 ft) from ocean floor to summit – 1,362 m (4,469 ft) taller than Mount Everest!

SOUTHER

TO DATE, IT IS THOUGHT THAT WE HAVE ONLY EXPLORED

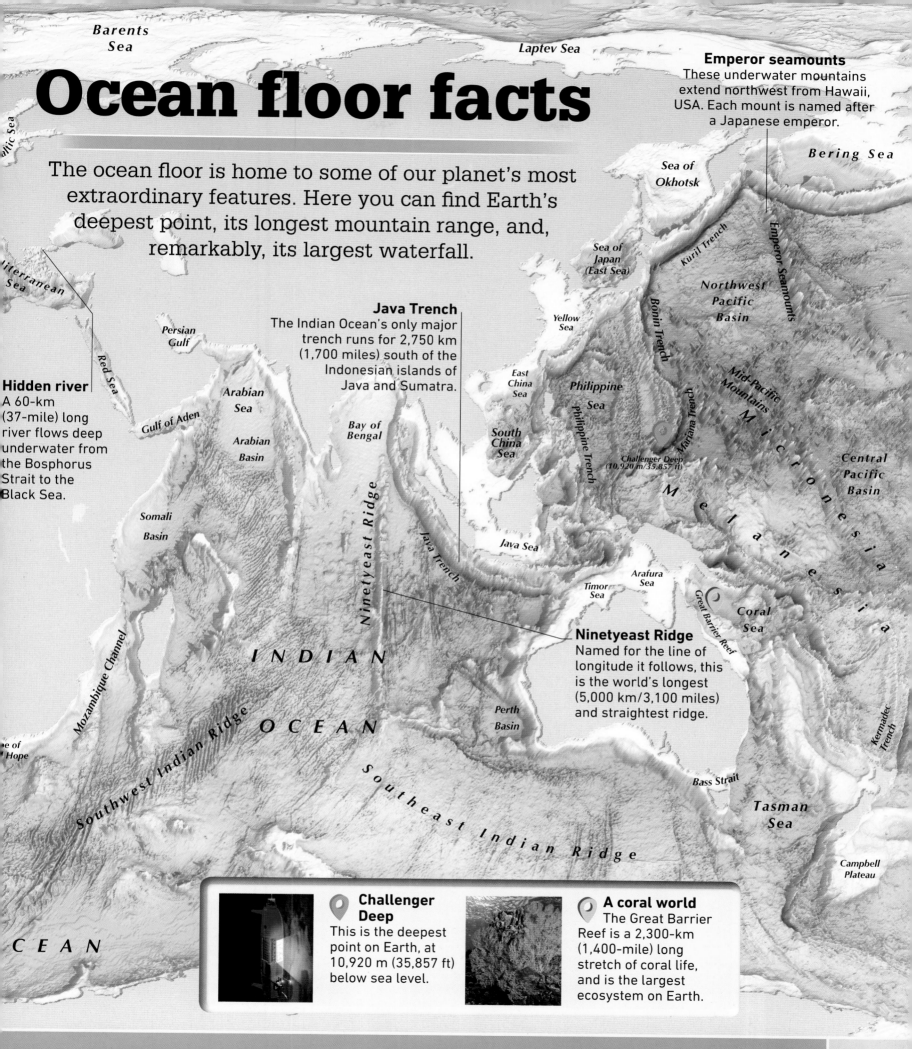

Ocean floor facts

The ocean floor is home to some of our planet's most extraordinary features. Here you can find Earth's deepest point, its longest mountain range, and, remarkably, its largest waterfall.

Emperor seamounts
These underwater mountains extend northwest from Hawaii, USA. Each mount is named after a Japanese emperor.

Java Trench
The Indian Ocean's only major trench runs for 2,750 km (1,700 miles) south of the Indonesian islands of Java and Sumatra.

Hidden river
A 60-km (37-mile) long river flows deep underwater from the Bosphorus Strait to the Black Sea.

Ninetyeast Ridge
Named for the line of longitude it follows, this is the world's longest (5,000 km/3,100 miles) and straightest ridge.

Barents Sea

Laptev Sea

Bering Sea

Baltic Sea

Mediterranean Sea

Sea of Okhotsk

Sea of Japan (East Sea)

Kuril Trench

Emperor Seamounts

Northwest Pacific Basin

Persian Gulf

Red Sea

Yellow Sea

Bonin Trench

Mid-Pacific Mountains

Central Pacific Basin

Gulf of Aden

Arabian Sea

East China Sea

Philippine Sea

Mariana Trench

Micronesia

Arabian Basin

Bay of Bengal

South China Sea

Philippine Trench

Challenger Deep (10,920 m/35,857 ft)

Melanesia

Somali Basin

Java Sea

Java Trench

Ninetyeast Ridge

Timor Sea

Arafura Sea

Great Barrier Reef

Coral Sea

INDIAN

OCEAN

Perth Basin

Bass Strait

Kermadec Trench

Mozambique Channel

Cape of Good Hope

Southwest Indian Ridge

Southeast Indian Ridge

Tasman Sea

Campbell Plateau

OCEAN

⌖ Challenger Deep
This is the deepest point on Earth, at 10,920 m (35,857 ft) below sea level.

⌖ A coral world
The Great Barrier Reef is a 2,300-km (1,400-mile) long stretch of coral life, and is the largest ecosystem on Earth.

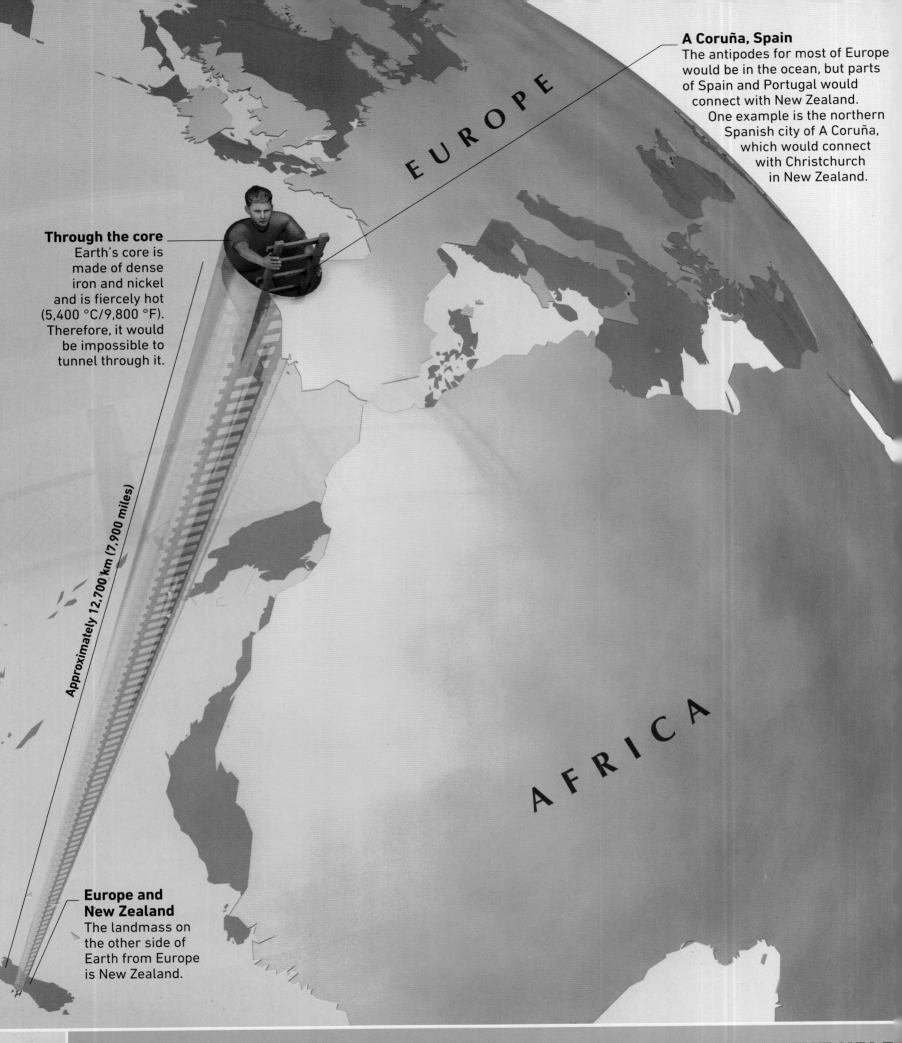

A Coruña, Spain
The antipodes for most of Europe would be in the ocean, but parts of Spain and Portugal would connect with New Zealand. One example is the northern Spanish city of A Coruña, which would connect with Christchurch in New Zealand.

EUROPE

Through the core
Earth's core is made of dense iron and nickel and is fiercely hot (5,400 °C/9,800 °F). Therefore, it would be impossible to tunnel through it.

Approximately 12,700 km (7,900 miles)

AFRICA

Europe and New Zealand
The landmass on the other side of Earth from Europe is New Zealand.

SO FAR, THE DEEPEST HOLE MADE IN EARTH'S SURFACE IS THE KOLA

Through Earth's core

If it were possible to drill a hole through Earth and come out on the other side, most of us would end up in the ocean. This is because most of Earth's surface is covered by sea. However, there are a few places where a city would link up to another city on the other side of the world.

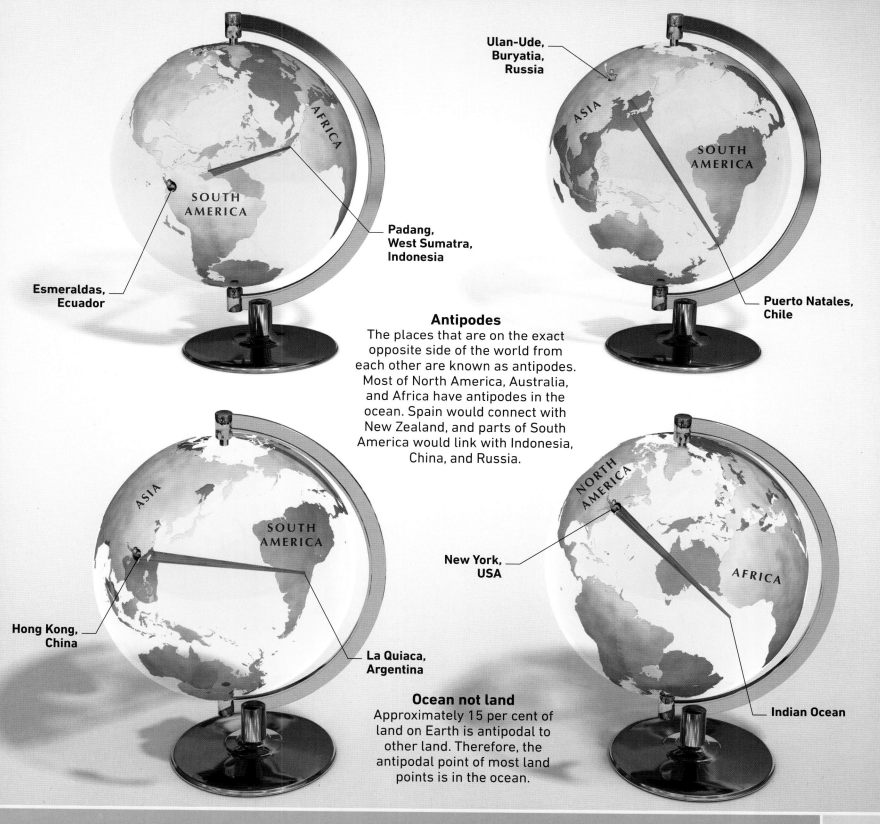

Ulan-Ude, Buryatia, Russia

Padang, West Sumatra, Indonesia

Esmeraldas, Ecuador

Puerto Natales, Chile

Antipodes
The places that are on the exact opposite side of the world from each other are known as antipodes. Most of North America, Australia, and Africa have antipodes in the ocean. Spain would connect with New Zealand, and parts of South America would link with Indonesia, China, and Russia.

Hong Kong, China

La Quiaca, Argentina

New York, USA

Indian Ocean

Ocean not land
Approximately 15 per cent of land on Earth is antipodal to other land. Therefore, the antipodal point of most land points is in the ocean.

Pole to Pole
Pangaea extends from the North Pole to the South Pole, so you can travel from pole to pole by land.

Western Europe
There is no Atlantic Ocean between Europe and North America.

Giant ocean
A single ocean called Panthalassa stretches across two-thirds of Earth.

North America
The US east coast borders Africa, with New York City alongside Mauritania.

Brazil
Brazil has no coastline. Its eastern boundary borders Africa.

Perfect fit
The east coast of South America and the west coast of Africa neatly fit together.

Central Pangaea
With weather systems unable to reach the interior parts of Pangaea, many countries would have been extremely hot during daytime and freezing at night. Rainfall would also have been rare.

GREENLAND

NORWAY SWEDEN FINLAND

RUSSIAN FEDERATION

ESTONIA
LATVIA
LITHUANIA
BELARUS

NETHERLANDS
DENMARK
POLAND
UKRAINE

CANADA

UNITED KINGDOM
GERMANY

IRELAND
BELGIUM

MOLDO
SLOVAKIA
HUNGARY
CZECH REPUBLIC
AUSTRIA
SWITZERLAND

FRANCE

UNITED STATES OF AMERICA

PORTUGAL
SPAIN

MOROCCO

ITALY

MEXICO

MAURITANIA
SENEGAL

ALGERIA

TUNISIA

GREECE

GUINEA-BISSAU
GAMBIA

TURKEY

VENEZUELA

SIERRA LEONE
GUINEA

MALI

LIBYA

COLOMBIA

LIBERIA
IVORY COAST

BURKINA FASO

NIGER

SYRIA

ECUADOR

GUYANA

GHANA
TOGO
BENIN

EGYPT
JORDAN
IRAQ

PERU

SURINAME
FRENCH GUIANA

NIGERIA

CHAD

SAUDI ARABIA

CAMEROON

BRAZIL

GABON

CENTRAL AFRICAN REPUBLIC

SUDAN

ERITREA

BOLIVIA

CONGO

DEMOCRATIC REPUBLIC OF THE CONGO

SOUTH SUDAN

UAE
YEMEN
OMA

ETHIOPIA

PARAGUAY

RWANDA
BURUNDI

UGANDA

SOMALIA

KENYA

PAKISTA

ARGENTINA
CHILE

URUGUAY

NAMIBIA

ANGOLA

TANZANIA

MADAGASCAR

INDIA

NEPA

ZAMBIA

MALAWI

BOTSWANA
ZIMBABWE

MOZAMBIQUE
SRI LANKA

BHUTAN

SOUTH AFRICA

BANGLADESH

SWAZILAND

LESOTHO

ANTARCTICA

A continent of countries

This is a map of what Earth probably looked like 270 million years ago when the landmasses were joined together forming a single supercontinent, called Pangaea. But there's one obvious addition – the map also features modern international borders showing where today's countries were located back then. Over 180 million years, the continents split apart and drifted over the planet.

Ancient landmass
The vast, single continent of Pangaea stretched from pole to pole and stayed intact for almost 160 million years.

PANGAEA

China
What is now eastern China was a separate landmass called Cathaysia. It collided with Pangaea millions of years later.

RUSSIAN FEDERATION

CHINA

NORTH KOREA
SOUTH KOREA
CHINA
VIETNAM
LAOS
THAILAND
CAMBODIA

THAILAND

INDONESIA

CHINA

AUSTRALIA

ANTARCTICA

India
India lies in the southern hemisphere, next to Antarctica. With the ocean to the east, India most likely enjoyed a warm and wet climate.

Australia
In Pangaea, it is possible to walk from Australia to the northern hemisphere.

Theory of Pangaea
The idea of the supercontinent was first proposed by German scientist Alfred Wegener in 1912. He noticed how the edges of the separate continents fitted together like pieces of a jigsaw puzzle, and claimed that the continents had drifted away from one another over hundreds of millions of years.

High sea level
Earth is much warmer, ice caps are slowly melting, and sea levels are at their highest, submerging low-lying areas across the world.

Atlantic Ocean
Over the course of the next 150 million years, one tectonic plate is pulled under another on the west side of the Atlantic. As a result, the Atlantic Ocean will shrink.

Amazon Sea
Once a thriving tropical rainforest, large parts of the Amazon Basin are now under the sea.

Expanding islands
The Falklands, South Georgia, and South Sandwich Island expand into a large island chain that stretches across the Atlantic Ocean.

Antarctica
The landmass drifts away from the South Pole and veers north. It will eventually meet Asia and close off the Indian Ocean.

North America
Land that used to be Southern and Baja California has drifted away to form North America's western mountain range.

NORTH AMERICA

SOUTH AMERICA

Future Earth

Earth's continents sit on tectonic plates that move on a sea of magma (molten lava) at speeds of between 1 and 10 cm (⅓ to 4 in) per year. Using geological clues, which reveal how these plates are moving, experts have predicted what Earth might look like in 100 million years.

IN 100 MILLION YEARS, EARTH'S ROTATION WILL HAVE SLOWED

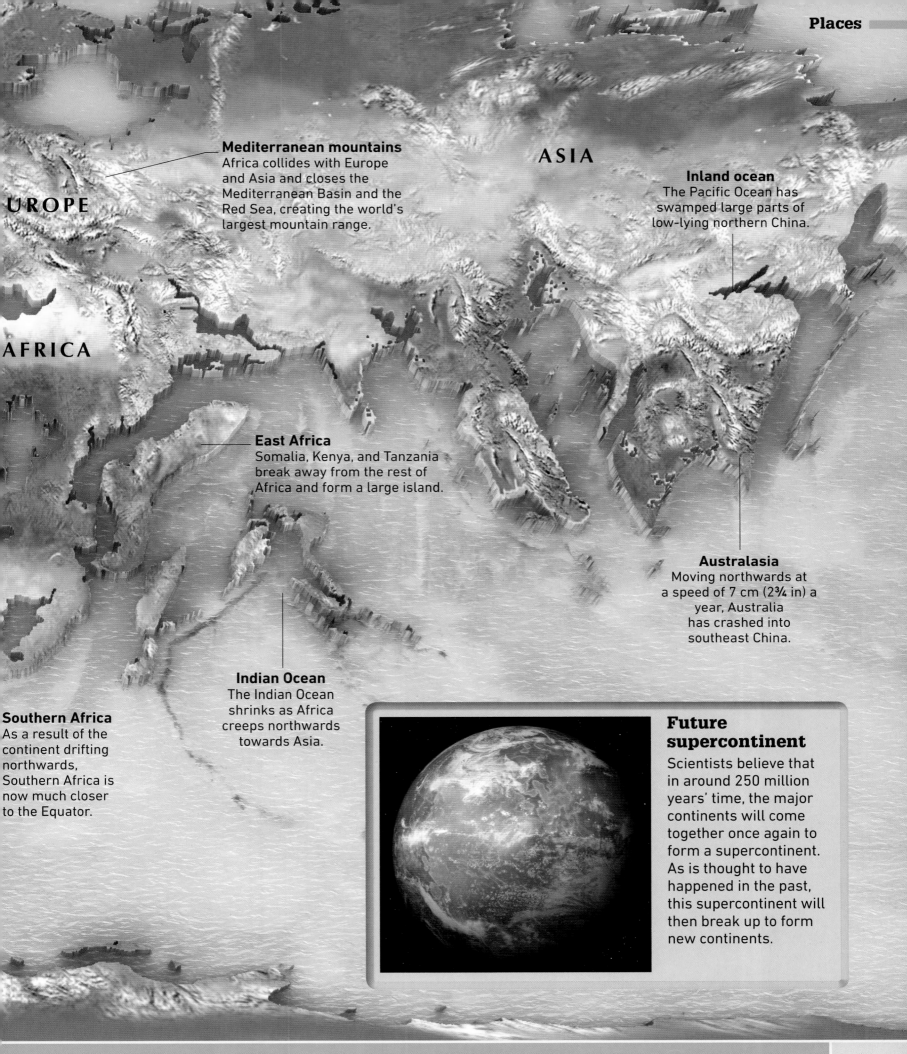

Mediterranean mountains
Africa collides with Europe and Asia and closes the Mediterranean Basin and the Red Sea, creating the world's largest mountain range.

ASIA

Inland ocean
The Pacific Ocean has swamped large parts of low-lying northern China.

UROPE

AFRICA

East Africa
Somalia, Kenya, and Tanzania break away from the rest of Africa and form a large island.

Australasia
Moving northwards at a speed of 7 cm (2¾ in) a year, Australia has crashed into southeast China.

Indian Ocean
The Indian Ocean shrinks as Africa creeps northwards towards Asia.

Southern Africa
As a result of the continent drifting northwards, Southern Africa is now much closer to the Equator.

Future supercontinent
Scientists believe that in around 250 million years' time, the major continents will come together once again to form a supercontinent. As is thought to have happened in the past, this supercontinent will then break up to form new continents.

People

Tomato time
Spain's La Tomatina festival started in the 1940s and has become the world's biggest food fight. On the last Wednesday of August, 20,000 people gather for an hour to throw truckloads of tomatoes at each other.

Canada
With fewer than 7 million children – less than one-fifth of its total population – Canada has the lowest proportion of children in North America.

USA
More than 74 million children live in the USA: the most of any country in North America.

Guatemala
Around 43 per cent of Guatemala's population is aged 0–17 – the highest proportion in North America.

Aruba
Just 24,000 children live on the Caribbean island of Aruba – the lowest number in North America.

NORTH AMERICA

Germany
With only 16 per cent of the population aged under 17, Germany has the lowest proportion of children in Europe.

Ireland
One-quarter of Ireland's population is aged 0–17: the highest proportion of children in Europe.

EUROPE

Malta
Malta has the lowest number of children in Europe – about 75,000.

Niger
More than 57 per cent of Niger's population under 18.

Nigeria
There are 91.5 million children in Nigeria: the most in any African country.

French Guiana
Nearly 40 per cent of French Guiana's population is aged 0–17 – the highest proportion in South America.

Brazil
With 56.8 million 0–17-year-olds, Brazil has more children than any other South American country.

SOUTH AMERICA

A world of children

There are about 2.3 billion children in the world. This map shows where they live, with the countries resized according to the number of children in each one. The biggest countries are those with the most children. Usually, the nations with the largest total populations have the most children; and those with the smallest have the fewest.

Children by continent
Just under one-third of the world's population is aged 0–17. More than half of them live in Asia, but Africa has the highest proportion of children compared to its total population.

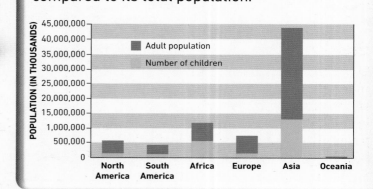

POPULATION (IN THOUSANDS)		
45,000,000		
40,000,000	■ Adult population	
35,000,000		
30,000,000	■ Number of children	
25,000,000		
20,000,000		
15,000,000		
1,000,000		
500,000		
0		

North America | South America | Africa | Europe | Asia | Oceania

Russia
One-fifth of all Europe's children live in Russia, which has 27.9 million under-18s – the highest number in Europe.

China
China has the world's biggest total population, with more than 1.4 billion people; but it has only the second-highest number of children (299.3 million).

Afghanistan
Asia's highest proportion of children can be found in Afghanistan: 52 per cent of the country's population of 34.1 million is aged 0–17.

Lucknow
India

Japan
Just 16 per cent of Japan's population is under 18. This is the joint-lowest proportion in Asia, along with Qatar and the UAE.

ASIA

India
India has more children than any other country in the world: 449.7 million under-18s live here, which is about one-third of the country's total population.

Micronesia
Micronesia has the fewest number of children in Asia, with just 43,000 under-18s.

AFRICA

Seychelles
The Seychelles has Africa's smallest population of children, with 24,000.

Maldives
The Maldive Islands have the fewest number of children in Asia, with 115,000.

AUSTRALASIA AND OCEANIA

Australia
While Australia has the most children of any country in Australasia and Oceania (5.3 million), it also has the lowest proportion: 22.5 per cent of its total population.

🗺 The world's biggest school

In places where there are many children, you need a big school. City Montessori School in Lucknow, India, has 55,000 pupils. One of its 20 campuses has 1,020 classrooms.

HMS *Bounty*

One of the most famous mutinies of all time took place on this British ship in 1789. A rebel lieutenant overthrew the captain and set him and his loyal sailors adrift in an overloaded boat. Despite a lack of supplies, those cast adrift survived and made it to Timor a few months later.

Ada Blackjack
Wrangel Island, 1921–23
This Inuit woman was the only member of a failed Canadian expedition to survive. She lived alone on a freezing Arctic island for two years.

Gonzalo de Vigo
Guam, 1522–26
Having deserted a round-the-world expedition, this Spanish sailor lived with native tribes until he was found by another ship.

Jesús Vidaña, Lucio Rendón, and Salvador Ordóñez
Mexico to Marshall Islands, 2005–06
Three fisherman were cast adrift when their boat ran out of fuel. They were rescued nine months later, having drifted across the Pacific Ocean.

Captain Oguri Jukichi
Japan to USA, 1813–15
When this sea captain's disabled ship landed in California, he became one of the first Japanese people to visit America.

Rolando Omongos
General Santos City, Philippines to New Britain Island, 2017
This 21-year-old was adrift for 56 days, living on raw fish, rainwater, and moss.

José Salvador Alvarenga
Mexico to Marshall Islands, 2012–14
This El Salvador man floated 10,800 km (6,700 miles) across the Pacific Ocean, staying alive for 438 days by drinking turtle blood and his own urine.

Uein Buranibwe and Temaei Tontaake
Kiribati to Marshall Islands, 2011
A GPS that ran out of batteries led these two men to float westwards to the Marshall Islands, where one of them discovered a long-lost uncle!

HMS *Bounty*
Tofua to Timor, 1789

Abraham Leeman van Sanwitz
Australia to Java, 1658
After losing sight of their ship in a storm, this captain and his crew were forced make a 21-day journey back to Java in a leaky rowing boat.

The crew of the *Rose-Noëlle*
South Island to Great Barrier Island, New Zealand, 1989
Four men became trapped drifting in an upside-down yacht after it was capsized by an enormous wave. After drifting for 119 days, they were finally rescued.

Robert Bogucki
Great Sandy Desert, Australia, 1999
On a spiritual quest, this American man wandered deep into the desert and was lost for 43 days.

Thomas Musgrave
Auckland Island to Stewart Island, 1864
Shipwrecked by bad weather, this captain and his crew were stranded for 18 months on a subantarctic island before heading out to seek rescue in a makeshift dinghy.

MOST PEOPLE CAN SURVIVE WITHOUT WATER

KEY
The icons on this map show the environment in which these dramatic stories of survival took place.

On an island

In the desert

At sea

Mauro Prosperi
Sahara Desert, 1994
While competing in a gruelling desert marathon, this Italian athlete lost his way during a sandstorm. He wandered 291 km (181 miles) off course before he was found nine days later.

Phillip Ashton
Roatán Island, Honduras, 1722
Fleeing into the jungle of a mysterious island to escape the pirates who had captured him, this American fisherman was finally rescued around 16 months later.

Steven Callahan
Canary Islands to Guadeloupe, 1982
This American sailor was forced to abandon ship. He was adrift on a life raft for 76 days and crossed the Atlantic Ocean before a fisherman rescued him.

Poon Lim
Brazilian coast, 1942
When his merchant ship was torpedoed, this steward was cast away on a raft and spent the longest time alone adrift at sea: 133 days.

Maurice and Maralyn Bailey
Panama to Galápagos Islands, 1973
This couple ate many sea creatures to stay alive, including six young sharks that they caught with safety pins and their bare hands.

Alexander Selkirk
Robinson Crusoe Island, 1704–09
Although he was not the first sailor to be stranded here, this British naval officer's story inspired the famous novel *Robinson Crusoe*.

Charles Barnard
Eagle Island, 1812–14
An American sea captain, he was treacherously marooned after the British sailed away in his ship.

Ernest Shackleton
Antarctica, 1915–16
This famous British explorer and his crew became trapped on floating ice after it cracked their ship's hull. They undertook an arduous 563-km (350-mile) journey north to find help.

Super survivors

Whether adrift in the ocean or deserted in the desert, these incredible survivors ended up stranded in some of the world's remotest places. While they waited for rescue, many had to resort to drastic measures to keep themselves alive.

FOR SIX OR SEVEN DAYS AT SEA.

What's in your kitchen?

A surprising number of everyday foods kept in the store cupboard or fridge contain substances that could be harmful if eaten in large quantities.

Rhubarb leaves (but not the stems) contain poisons called oxalates that may damage the kidneys.

Nutmeg is poisonous if eaten in large amounts. Symptoms of poisoning include hallucinations.

Almonds, both sweet and bitter types, contain the poison cyanide, but shop-bought nuts are safe.

Honey can contain tiny amounts of a toxin that may cause botulism (severe poisoning), which can be fatal.

Tuna may be high in mercury, a poisonous metal that can cause serious health problems.

Potatoes seem quite harmless, but a poison is found in any that are green or sprouting.

Toxic treats

Approach these dishes with caution, because just one mouthful could be deadly. Some contain poisons and others look or smell really bad. So they all need to be prepared very carefully by people who know exactly what they are doing. Even then they might still prove fatal!

Hákarl *Iceland*
Rotting shark meat, or hákarl, is a famous Icelandic dish. Shark flesh can be dangerous to eat, as it often contains high levels of toxic chemicals, such as the waste product urea.

Casu Marzu *Italy*
While this Sardinian sheep's cheese is ripening, fly maggots are left to develop inside it. The cheese, eaten with the live maggots still in it, is said to cause stomach problems.

Ackee fruit *Jamaica*
Before the pods ripen, turn red, and open naturally, the ackee contains a poison that can cause vomiting, a coma, or even death.

Though **scorpions** have a **venomous sting**, they are **safe to eat** if they have been **cooked**.

ALL FOOD AND DRINK CAN BE TOXIC IF EATEN IN EXCESSIVE AMOUNTS.

Fugu (puffer fish) *Japan*
One of the most high-risk foods in the world, parts of this fish contain a poison a thousand times deadlier than cyanide.

Sannakji *South Korea*
A small octopus is cut up alive to dip into sauces. Served whole, the octopus has been known to choke diners with its still-moving tentacles.

Locusts *Israel*
To get rid of these crop-destroying insects, Israeli farmers have come up with a unique method of pest control: deep-frying the locusts and eating them.

Blood clams *China*
Although widely eaten, these shellfish can be full of viruses and bacteria that lead to hepatitis (liver disease), typhoid, and dysentery. A few people have even died.

Fesikh *Egypt*
Eaten at the Egyptian spring festival, fesikh is a dish of fish that has been fermented for up to a year. If not prepared properly, it can be a health risk.

Tarantulas *Cambodia*
Deep-fried spiders are a popular street snack in Cambodia. The animal's body hairs cause allergies, so are singed off before cooking.

Pangium edule *Singapore*
The large, brown "football fruit" can kill if eaten raw, as it contains lethal hydrogen cyanide. Boiling and fermenting removes the poison.

Bat soup *Palau*
Palau islanders eat them in soup, but bats are also eaten grilled and barbecued in Southeast Asia. Bat meat, however, can carry disease.

African bullfrog
Namibia
Although considered a local food treat, this bullfrog has toxins in its body that can be poisonous to humans.

Careful preparation

Chefs who prepare the dangerous puffer fish or fugu, must train for two years before they take a test, which a third of candidates fail. Just a sliver of the fish's toxic organs would kill a diner.

Fantastic food facts

Everyone has a favourite food, but how many people have a favourite food fact? Feast your eyes on this buffet of strange stories and tantalizing titbits about the everyday things we eat.

Bog butter
Ireland
Prehistoric people used to store their butter in bogs to preserve it. A 10-kg (22-lb) chunk was unearthed in Ireland in 2011. It was more than 2,000 years old.

Accidental ice-lolly
California, USA
This frozen favourite was accidentally created by an 11-year-old boy, when, in 1905, his soda ingredients froze in cold weather.

Maple syrup heist
Quebec, Canada
Maple syrup is worth about US$1,300 a barrel. In 2012, a gang stole $18 million-worth of it, refilling the barrels in the storehouse with water.

Chocolate money
Central America
For centuries, cocoa beans were a coveted currency for the Maya and Aztec civilizations. They were traded for a range of goods.

Coca-Cola character
Atlanta, Georgia, USA
The jolly Santa Claus figure we see at Christmas today was made popular by the Coca-Cola Company in the 1930s, when they featured him in their adverts.

Potato time
Western South America
The Incas used the length of time it took to boil a potato as a measurement of time.

Miracle fruit
West Africa
Any food can become a sweet treat after eating a miracle fruit. Despite its low sugar content, this berry transforms the taste of sour foods so they become super sweet.

The **Romans** ate lots of **unusual foods**, including blood pudding, fish guts, and **flamingo tongue**

IN 1807, A FRENCH FOOD CRITIC PROPOSED A RECIPE FOR "THE ROAST

Tender Tartar tartare
Eastern Europe
It is said that eating raw "steak tartare" comes from Tartar warriors, who put meat under their saddles to tenderize it with the horse's sweat. However, they may have done this to protect the horse from sores instead.

Flight food
Plane food might seem plain, but food actually tastes different up in the air. Due to the pressure inside the aeroplane cabin, your ability to taste sweet and salty foods can be reduced by 30 per cent. Airlines compensate for this by using stronger flavours.

Yoghurt makers
Central Asia
When herdsmen in 6000 BCE started carrying milk around in bags made of animal stomachs, they accidentally created yoghurt.

Spices
Tropical countries
In warm countries, spices aren't only used for taste; they also help preserve food in the heat.

Seaweed secrets
Japan
Seaweed-wrapped sushi owes its success to a British woman – Dr Kathleen Drew-Baker – who discovered how to grow the crop more reliably. She is celebrated in Uto, Japan, as the "Mother of the Sea".

Tea myths
China
Many legends surround the origin of tea. One story tells how tea trees grew from the severed eyelids of the monk Bodhidharma, who cut them off to punish himself when he fell asleep during meditation.

acred onions
ncient Egypt
o the ancient Egyptians nions were a egetable worthy f worship. They ven buried ome with heir pharaohs.

Watermelon
Africa
Watermelons are only red because of "plant breeding". Careful farming changed the fruit from being green and bitter to red and tasty.

Elephant dung coffee
Thailand
Some of the world's most expensive (and allegedly tastiest) coffee is made from beans that have been eaten by an elephant and then expelled in its poo.

Super salt

In ancient and medieval times, salt was valued as highly as gold. More than just a flavouring, this essential food preservative is still used today, in "curing" dried fish, for example.

Glowing pork chops
Australia
In 2005, people were spooked by the discovery of glowing pork in their fridges. This effect turned out to be caused by bacteria.

Duckmaster
Tennessee, USA
An employee at a Tennessee hotel carries a cane and trains the venue's ducks to march through the lobby.

Iceberg mover
Arctic region
When drifting icebergs float too close to oil rigs, these employees must tow them away.

Crack filler
South Dakota, USA
This job involves scaling down Mount Rushmore on ropes, to seal up cracks in the presidents' faces carved into the mountain.

Swan marker
London, UK
Advising on swan welfare and organizing an annual swan census are this royal official's main duties.

Coconut safety engineer
US Virgin Islands
This is a job of dizzying heights – involving climbing treetops to retrieve coconuts before they fall.

St Mark's Guardians
Venice, Italy
These stewards patrol this famous square to watch out for tourists breaking the rules.

Dog-surfing instructor
California, USA A teacher who shows pooches how to paddle is one of the staff positions at a pet-friendly Californian hotel.

Sloth nanny
Costa Rica
This carer must be far from slothful, as sloth babies need feeding four times a day.

Zebra crossing assistant
Bolivia
Volunteers dressed in zebra costumes encourage drivers and pedestrians to follow the rules in a light-hearted way.

Robot hotel
At the Henn-na Hotel in Sasebo, Japan, almost all the staff are robots, including the porters, the concierge, and even a dinosaur receptionist. However, these machines are still unable to make beds.

Many golf clubs employ **professional divers** to fish out golf balls from the water.

PROFESSIONAL ODOUR SNIFFERS TEST BEAUTY PRODUCTS SUCH AS THE

Professional sleeper
Helsinki, Finland
Advertised in 2013, this job involved testing every single one of a hotel's 35 rooms.

Animal jobs
There are many peculiar professions that involve working with animals – for the animals' benefit, or for ours. Tasting dog food and training animals for films are among the wackier jobs, but others can be very dangerous.

A big-cat dentist must reach inside the mouths of lions and tigers to check their teeth for any problems.

Milking snakes is a life-threatening, but important, job. Antidotes to snake bites are made from the venom.

LEGO® Master Builder
Billund, Denmark
A few specially selected individuals get to achieve this job title by constructing brilliant LEGO® builds.

strich babysitter
South Africa
reaking up fights tween these birds a key responsibility in this role.

Chicken sexer *Japan*
Telling male and female chickens apart is no easy business. Japan has a special training school for this tricky type of work.

Professional mourner *China*
These actors deliver dramatic displays of grief in order to show that the deceased was loved.

Ear cleaner *India*
Armed with just cotton wool and a steel needle, these practitioners seek trade on the streets of Delhi. However, this waxy business is waning.

Professional hitchhiker
Jakarta, Indonesia
Drivers wishing to beat the traffic in this busy city may pick up an extra passenger, allowing them to use the fast lane.

Crazy careers

If the daily grind isn't for you, take a look at the globe's strangest jobs. Whether caring, creative, or practical, these varied vocations are all worlds apart from the normal nine-to-five job.

Island caretaker
Hamilton Island, Australia
Touted as "the best job in the world", the caretaker's role is to explore and promote the island.

Frog Festival

This three-day fair that takes place every year in Louisiana, USA, features frog jumping and races; and the crowning of (human) Frog Festival Queens.

Up Helly Aa
Shetland Islands, UK

Cheese-rolling Festival
Gloucestershire, UK

El Colacho *Castrillo De Murcia, Spain*

UFO Festival
New Mexico, USA

Frog Festival
Louisiana, USA

Night of the Radishes
Oaxaca, Mexico

Twine Ball Day
Minnesota, USA
This day celebrates what was the world's biggest twine ball.

Carnival of Ivrea
Turin, Italy
People hurl oranges at each other at this fruity festival.

Underwater Music Festival *Florida, USA*
Divers play mock instruments while listening to music.

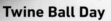

Bolas de Fuego
Nejapa, El Salvador
At the "balls of fire" festival, teams throw fireballs at each other.

Argungu Fishing Festival
Argungu, Nigeria
Thousands compete to land the biggest fish in one hour.

Lumberjack Festival
Cape Town, South Africa
The "Lumber Games" include axe-throwing and log-hurling.

UFO Festival

A celebration of aliens, held in Roswell – the site of the USA's most-debated alien encounter. Many still believe a UFO crashed there in 1947.

Night of the Radishes

Mexicans celebrate the historical practice of sculpting radishes to advertise them.

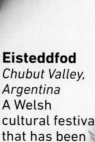
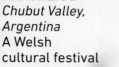

Eisteddfod
Chubut Valley, Argentina
A Welsh cultural festival that has been transplanted to South America.

El Colacho

This Spanish festival is also known as baby jumping, because men dressed as the devil (*colacho*) jump over babies to rid them of sin.

THERE ARE FESTIVALS IN SPAIN AT WHICH PEOPLE THROW TOMATOES

Up Helly Aa
The climax of this Viking-themed fire festival is the burning of a longboat. This tradition started 1,000 years after Vikings invaded the Shetland Islands, in the north of the UK.

Busójárás *Mohács, Hungary*
People dress in scary masks to celebrate the end of winter.

Boryeong Mud Festival
Daecheon Beach, South Korea

Monkey Buffet Festival
Lopburi, Thailand

Naki Sumo
Tokyo, Japan
At the "baby crying competition", sumo wrestlers gently make babies cry to rid them of demons.

Golden Gumboot Festival
Tully, Queensland, Australia
This festival includes the "Gumboot Games", celebrating the town's tropical, rainy climate.

Far-out festivals

There are some curious celebrations in the world. A ball of string, cheese, and a wellington boot are all excuses for a fun day out; while babies are jumped over or made to cry in traditional ceremonies.

Cheese-rolling Festival
Competitors hurtle 183 m (200 yards) down a steep hill in England in pursuit of a wheel of cheese. Many people are injured in the attempt, but the winner keeps the cheese.

Mud Festival
Millions of visitors try the mud baths, mud slides, mud obstacle course, and more muddy things at this South Korean festival, which also advertises cosmetics made from the mineral-rich mud.

Monkey Buffet Festival
At this event in Thailand, people feed the town's 2,000 macaques with huge displays of fruit, cakes, and sweets.

West Coast Pumpkin Regatta
Oregon, USA
Contestants in fancy dress race across a lake paddling giant pumpkins in a series of wacky races.

Pillow Fight League
Toronto, Canada
This tongue-in-cheek, semi-professional league sees women do battle armed only with pillows.

Sporthocking
Germany
Described as a cross between skateboarding and sitting, competitors perform mad antics with a specially designed stool.

Kaiju Big Battel
Boston, USA
Wrestlers dressed up as monsters engage in ferocious mock fights.

Toe Wrestling Championships
Ashbourne, UK
Similar to arm wrestling but with toes, wrestlers descend on the English town of Ashbourne every year to decide the sport's world champion.

Chess boxing
The Netherlands
Competitors in this extraordinary sport take part in alternate rounds of chess and boxing.

"To Hell's Gate on a Wheelbarrow"
Kenya
Competitors take part in wheelbarrow races of differing lengths in Kenya's Hell's Gate National Park to raise money for conservation.

Footvolley
Brazil
This sport, half football, half beach volleyball, can be played on any surface, but sand is best.

360-Ball
South Africa
This racquet sport is played in a round court, and sees players from two teams hit the ball into a central dish.

Wackiest world sports

Good sport is made up of fun, thrills, and maybe a touch of danger. The quirky events shown here add sheer craziness as well, involving everything from paddling pumpkin boats to hurling cowpats.

Quidditch
Wizard Harry Potter's favourite sport has reached the non-magic world. Riding brooms, but with feet firmly on the ground, teams shoot goals and chase a runner who carries the Snitch in a sock.

Wife-carrying
Finland
The Wife-Carrying World Championships have been held in Finland every year since 1995.

Extreme ironing
This highly risky sport involves ironing clothes in unlikely and dangerous locations, such as at the top of a mountain, while skiing or snowboarding, or on a fast-moving boat.

Yubi lakpi
Manipur, India
Meaning "coconut snatching", this seven-a-side sport is a cross between rugby and football.

Panjat pinang
Indonesia
This traditional Indonesian sport sees contestants try to climb a greasy pole to claim the wheel-full of prizes at the top.

Robot jockeys
Middle East
Lightweight robot riders are slowly replacing human jockeys in the Middle Eastern sport of camel racing.

Bo-taoshi
Japan
In this dangerous sport, the defensive team has to stop the attacking team from toppling a 3–4.8-m (10–16-ft) pole.

Moonrock Throwing Championships
Queensland, Australia
This annual festival in the Australian outback sees competitors throw special rocks, called Moonrocks (which are not from the moon), as far as they can.

Henley-on-Todd Regatta
Alice Springs, Australia
This annual "boat" race is held on the dried-out bed of the Todd River in Alice Springs in Australia's Northern Territory.

Teams of **divers** have taken the sport of **extreme ironing underwater**.

Rural Games
Palmerston North, New Zealand
This annual event sees contestants take part in events such as barrel racing, cowpat hurling, and sheep shearing.

Chain of Craters Road *Hawaii, USA* This spectacular Hawaiian road passes through lava fields and volcanic craters.

White Rim Road *Utah, USA*

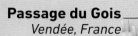

Capulin Volcano Road *New Mexico, USA* A 3.2-km (2-mile) road spirals around this extinct volcano.

Trollstigen Mountain Road *Rauma, Norway* This 55-km (34-mile) road has 11 hairpin bends.

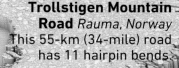

Lindisfarne Causeway *Lindisfarne, UK* This ancient road disappears twice a day at high tide.

Passage du Gois *Vendée, France* This causeway is only accessible at low tide.

Winston Churchill Avenue *Gibraltar*

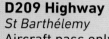

D209 Highway *St Barthélemy* Aircraft pass only a few feet above cars travelling on this road.

📍 **White Rim Road**

This 161-km (100-mile) off-road route in Utah, USA, is famous for its steep drops and scenic beauty.

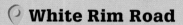

North Yungas Road *La Paz, Bolivia*

Highway SC-390 *Brazil* This narrow, zig-zag road is found in the Serra do Rio do Rastro mountain range in southern Brazil.

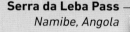

Stelvio Pass *South Tyrol and Sondrio, Italy* One of the highest mountain passes in Europe, this hair-raising road has more than 40 bends.

Serra da Leba Pass *Namibe, Angola*

📍 **North Yungas Road**

This 69-km (43-mile) track in Bolivia has been voted the most dangerous road in the world.

Sani Pass *KwaZulu-Natal, South Africa* This mountain pass reaches an elevation of 2,873 m (9,425 ft) and connects the South African province of KwaZulu-Natal with the country of Lesotho.

Stretching **47,958 km** (29,800 miles), the **Pan-American Highway** is the world's longest road.

📍 **Winston Churchill Avenue**

The main road connecting Gibraltar with Spain runs straight across Gibraltar Airport's runway.

KEY
These signs explain why the roads on this map are particularly dangerous.

 Contains many hairpins

 Affected by planes

 Covered at high tide

 Straight road

 Steep drops off the side

 Passes near to volcano

 Steep slope

Babusar Pass
Kaghan Valley, Pakistan
Reaching an elevation of 4,175 m (13,697 ft), this Himalayan road connects the Kaghan Valley with the Karakoram Highway.

Fairy Meadows Road
Gilgit-Baltistan, Pakistan
This 16.2-km (10-mile) gravel track is only as wide as a car and has no barriers.

Old Kunyi Road
Yunnan, China
This extraordinary road has 21 hairpins in just 2.1 km (1³⁄₁₀ miles).

Three Level Zig-Zag Road
Sikkim, India
There are more than 100 hairpin bends in this Himalayan mountain road.

Bayburt D915 road
Soganli Mountain, Turkey No barriers plus terrifying drops make this a truly hair-raising road.

6 Lawdar, Yemen
his 52.1-km (32²⁄₅-mile) asphalt road in entral Yemen contains 34 hairpin bends.

Guoliang Tunnel
Henan, China

24-Zig Road *Qinglong, China* This 24-hairpin road in southwest China was built just before World War Two.

⦿ Serra da Leba Pass
This mountain road in Angola drops 1,845 m (6,053 ft) in just over 10 km (6¹⁄₅ miles).

⦿ Guoliang Tunnel
This extraordinary road is carved along the side of and through a mountain in China.

⦿ Skippers Canyon Road
A 26.6-km (16½-mile) road cut into the side of a cliff face in New Zealand.

Hazardous highways

Eyre Highway
Australia
This highway in southern Australia includes the country's longest stretch of straight road – 145.6 km (91¹⁄₁₀ miles). It's enough to send drivers to sleep.

Baldwin Street
Dunedin, New Zealand
The world's steepest residential street has an incline of 19 degrees.

Skippers Canyon Road
South Island, New Zealand

f you're looking for a nice, relaxing road rip, then you should avoid these roads. From steep, barrier-less slopes and sharp bends to the threat of incoming tides, volcanoes, and even planes, these are some of the world's most hazardous highways.

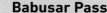
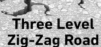

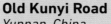

Switzerland
In some residences in this country, it is forbidden to flush the toilet after 10pm, to avoid disturbing the neighbours.

Bathtime rules
Etobicoke, Canada
It is unlawful to fill a bathtub with more than 9 cm (3½ in) of water before taking a bath in this suburb of Toronto.

No clowning around
Hood River, Oregon, USA
Juggling without a licence is prohibited in this US town.

Shoe safety
Spain
It is an offence to drive a vehicle wearing flip-flops or sandals in this country.

Hold fire
Florida, USA
Passing wind in a public place after 6pm on Thursdays is strictly prohibited in this state.

No freewheeling
Mexico
In this country, it is illegal for cyclists to lift their feet off the pedals while riding their bike.

Law of the land

Rules and regulations exist in every country, but some are stranger than others. Many of these unusual laws still stand today, while others were in the law books until very recently.

Pedal power
Brazil
Inmates of one prison in this country can reduce their jail time by pedalling a special bike that helps power the city's lights.

Nature for all
Sweden's *Allemansrätten* law grants people access to all the country's natural spaces. With the exception of protected areas, people are free to camp in any field, swim in any lake, or roam in any park. In fact, it is illegal to put up a "no trespassing" sign.

Keep dancing
Argentina
Official tango clubs in this country are regulated and must play more tango music than all other forms of music combined.

HUNDREDS OF YEARS AGO IN TURKEY, A WIFE COULD DIVORCE HER

Parking problems
Finland
Police here used to be able to deflate the tyres of any car that was illegally parked.

Car wash
Russia
Among Russia's driving laws is one that deems it illegal to drive a dirty car.

No sandcastles
Eraclea, Italy
In this small city near Venice, it is illegal to build sandcastles on the beach.

Family duty
China
Since 2013, it is compulsory for adults in China to visit their parents regularly.

Cold case
Japan
Putting ice cream in anyone's mailbox carries a maximum prison sentence of five years in this country.

Photo permits
Chad
It is against the law to take photographs in this country without obtaining a permit first.

Flying licence
India
According to the Indian Aircraft Act of 1934, a permit is required to fly a kite.

Attention!
China
To reduce road traffic accidents in Huangping province, China, children must stop and salute any passing cars.

Sticky mess
Singapore
In order to keep the streets clean, the sale of gum is prohibited in this city.

Bare hair
Madagascar
At one point it was against the law for pregnant women to wear hats in this island nation.

Forbidden fruit
Indonesia
The stinky durian fruit is banned from buses, subways, hotels, and airports in this country. If you have ever smelled one, you'll know why!

Don't sit too close
South Africa
An old law prohibited young people in bathing suits from sitting less than 30.5 cm (12 in) apart.

The **French town** of Granville has banned **elephants** from the beach.

Light bulb law
Victoria, Australia
For a brief period in this state, only a qualified electrician was allowed to change a light bulb.

National Mustard Museum
Wisconsin, USA
This museum contains 6,000 varieties of mustard and has mustard memorabilia from 70 countries.

Pig Museum
Stuttgart, Germany
This museum, in a former slaughterhouse, has 25 rooms of pig-related artefacts.

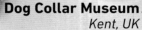

Dog Collar Museum
Kent, UK
This museum houses a collection of ornate pet accessories dating from the 15th to the 20th centuries.

Kansas Barbed Wire Museum
Kansas, USA
A museum that honours barbed wire, also known as "Devil's Rope".

International Banana Museum *California, USA*
This museum is home to a collection of 20,000 banana artefacts, from toys and socks to soap and perfume.

Vampire Museum
Paris, France
This Paris museum shows vampire paraphernalia including crossbows, masks, and a mummified cat.

Canadian Potato Museum
Prince Edward Island, Canada
This agricultural museum roots for the potato, featuring farm machinery and the world's biggest potato sculpture.

The Fossil Museum
Villa de Leyva, Colombia
A museum built around a 7-m (23-ft) long, 115-million-year-old Kronosaurus fossil, which was discoverd here in 1977.

Madcap museums

Tired of touring? Bored of the beach? Take a trip instead to these curious collections from single-minded curators who are dedicated to displaying strange stuff. Whether it's barbed wire or toilets, there's enough out there to satisfy even the most curious minds.

There are about **55,000** museums around the world.

Strange on the outside
It's not just the contents of museums that could be classified as weird – some of the buildings are deliberately eye-catching too.

Kunsthaus This modern-art gallery in Graz, Austria, is described as "biomorphic", which means based on life-forms.

IN 2017, A 100-KG (220-LB) GOLD COIN WORTH £3.6 MILLION

Yuri Detochkin Car Theft Museum
Moscow, Russia
Named for a 1960s TV comedy character who stole cars, this museum traces the history of one of Russia's most common crimes.

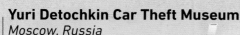

Teddy Bear Museum
Jeju-do, South Korea
In this museum's Art Hall, bears are arranged to recreate famous paintings such as the *Mona Lisa*.

Sulabh International Museum of Toilets
New Delhi, India
This museum tells the 4,500-year-old tale of toilet evolution.

China Watermelon Museum
Beijing, China
This fruity tribute is located near to one of the world's biggest watermelon-producing regions.

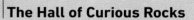

Avanos Hair Museum
Avanos, Turkey
Locks of hair from more than 16,000 women adorn the walls of a cave in a pottery shop.

The Hall of Curious Rocks
Saitama, Japan
This museum exhibits more than 1,700 rare rocks, many of which look like faces of celebrities and religious icons.

...mberley Mine Museum
...mberley, South Africa
...s open-air recreation of
...9th-century mining
...wn is next to the
...g Hole" — a 215-m
...5-ft) deep
...mond mine.

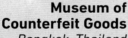

Kuching Cat Museum
Kuching, Malaysia
In Malay, *kucing* means "cat", and this similarly-named city is home to a museum that has a collection of 4,000 feline figurines and art.

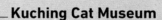

Museum of Counterfeit Goods
Bangkok, Thailand
Housed in a law office, this museum of 4,000 items aims to show people that fakes and forgeries will be found out!

National Wool Museum
Geelong, Australia
Located in a city once known as "the wool centre of the world", this museum knits together the history of wool in Australia.

Sock World
Hokitika, New Zealand
This sock shop contains what's thought to be a unique collection of antique circular sock-knitting machines.

Wonderworks This Orlando, USA, attraction claims its ...ilding was a science lab in the ...ermuda Triangle...

Oscar Niemeyer Museum This eye-shaped gallery in Curitiba, Brazil, is named for the artistic architect who designed it.

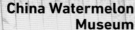

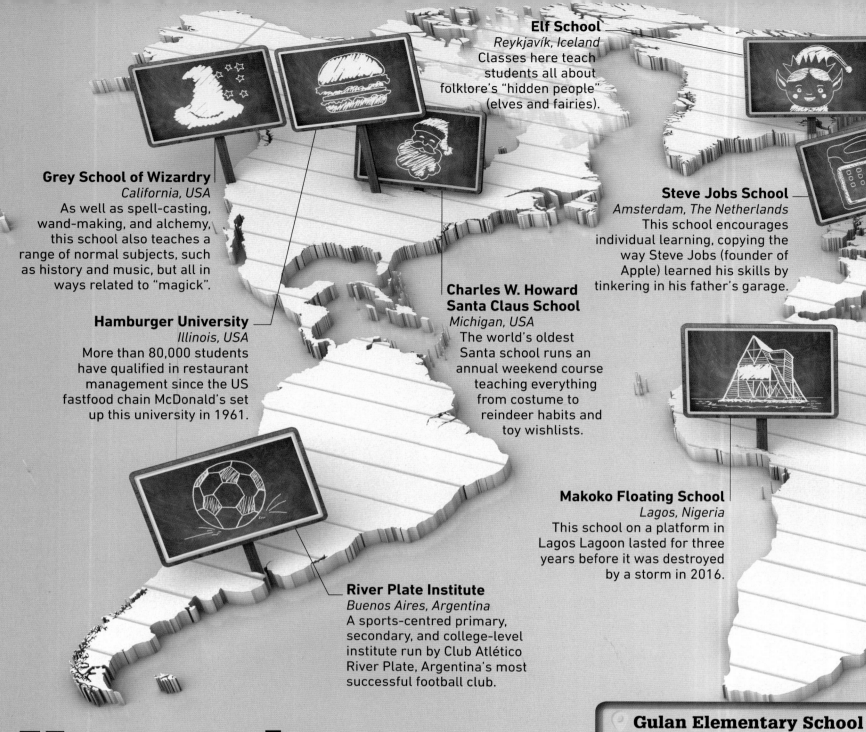

Elf School
Reykjavík, Iceland
Classes here teach students all about folklore's "hidden people" (elves and fairies).

Grey School of Wizardry
California, USA
As well as spell-casting, wand-making, and alchemy, this school also teaches a range of normal subjects, such as history and music, but all in ways related to "magick".

Steve Jobs School
Amsterdam, The Netherlands
This school encourages individual learning, copying the way Steve Jobs (founder of Apple) learned his skills by tinkering in his father's garage.

Hamburger University
Illinois, USA
More than 80,000 students have qualified in restaurant management since the US fastfood chain McDonald's set up this university in 1961.

Charles W. Howard Santa Claus School
Michigan, USA
The world's oldest Santa school runs an annual weekend course teaching everything from costume to reindeer habits and toy wishlists.

Makoko Floating School
Lagos, Nigeria
This school on a platform in Lagos Lagoon lasted for three years before it was destroyed by a storm in 2016.

River Plate Institute
Buenos Aires, Argentina
A sports-centred primary, secondary, and college-level institute run by Club Atlético River Plate, Argentina's most successful football club.

Unusual schools

For an education that's different to the norm, look no further than these schools and classes. Some have specialist curriculums, while others are unique because of their buildings or location.

Gulan Elementary School
This school, in Yu An county, Sichuan, China, is located halfway up a cliff. The school's pupils have to negotiate a path only 41 cm (16 in) wide at its narrowest point just to get there.

Egalia Preschool
Stockholm, Sweden
Children in this nursery develop likes and dislikes without any influences based on their gender. No one is called "he" or "she", but everyone is called "they".

Nomadic schools
Yakutia, Russia
Around 180 children are taught in 13 schools that follow the migrations of deer-herders around Yakutia in Siberia, Russia.

Kyiv Academy of Circus and Variety Arts *Kyiv, Ukraine*
More than just a "clown school", this university has been teaching music and theatre as well as circus arts since 1961.

Snake-charming school
Gujarat, India
Children from the Vadi tribe – who are traditional snake charmers – are taught skills in snake charming and snake care from the age of two.

Gulan Elementary School
Yu An, China

Mobile Learning
Pakistan
This United Nations project educates girls at home via their phones.

Green School
Bali, Indonesia
Pupils at this school learn how to look after the environment.

It costs **£86,000** per year to attend
Institut Le Rosey,
Switzerland – the **world's most expensive school**.

School of the Air
Alice Springs, Australia
This school for children living in remote areas conducts classes over the Internet. Lessons used to be held using walkie-talkies.

KEY
This map features a mix of formal schools and universities, and informal education such as evening classes.

▢ School
▢ University
▢ Informal class

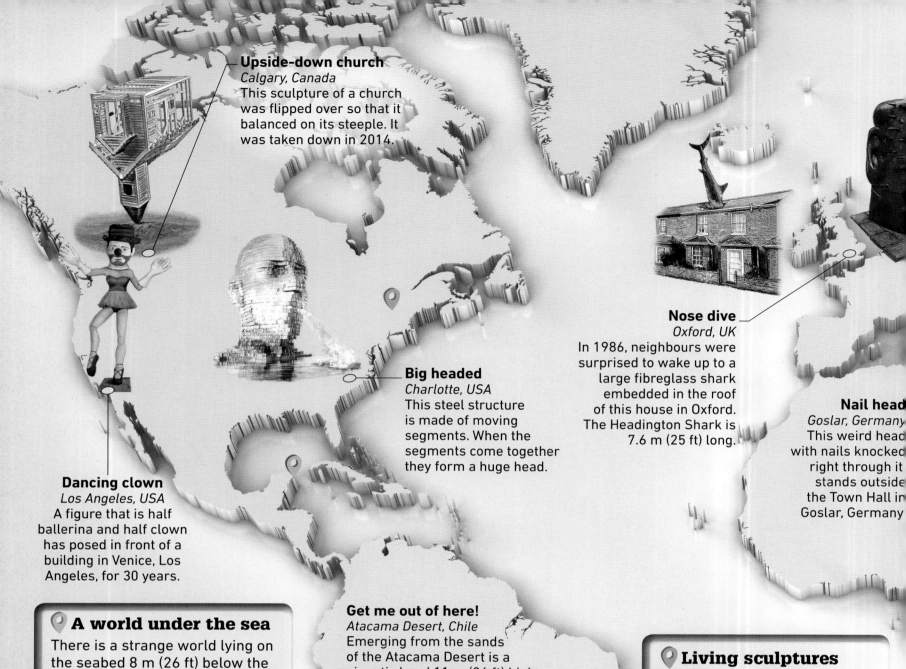

Upside-down church
Calgary, Canada
This sculpture of a church was flipped over so that it balanced on its steeple. It was taken down in 2014.

Dancing clown
Los Angeles, USA
A figure that is half ballerina and half clown has posed in front of a building in Venice, Los Angeles, for 30 years.

Big headed
Charlotte, USA
This steel structure is made of moving segments. When the segments come together they form a huge head.

Nose dive
Oxford, UK
In 1986, neighbours were surprised to wake up to a large fibreglass shark embedded in the roof of this house in Oxford. The Headington Shark is 7.6 m (25 ft) long.

Nail head
Goslar, Germany
This weird head with nails knocked right through it stands outside the Town Hall in Goslar, Germany.

A world under the sea
There is a strange world lying on the seabed 8 m (26 ft) below the Caribbean Sea in Cancún, Mexico. There are over 500 sculptures made by British artist Jason deCaires Taylor set on the seabed. Eventually coral will grow over them and form a new reef.

Get me out of here!
Atacama Desert, Chile
Emerging from the sands of the Atacama Desert is a gigantic hand 11 m (36 ft) high.

Living sculptures
The Botanical Gardens in Montreal, Canada, received some unusual sculptures for a competition in 2013. They were made from colourful plants, shaped into creatures, including earth spirits, birds, lemurs, and gorillas.

It's a Posankka
Turku, Finland
Sitting near the University of Turku, Finland, is a strange creature that is half marzipan pig (*possu* in Finnish) and half rubber duck (*ankka* in Finnish).

Melting cow
Budapest, Hungary
Displayed in Budapest, Hungary, in 2006, this bright blue cow appeared to be melting into the pavement like a giant ice lolly.

Kissing dinosaurs
Erenhot, China
Reaching out across a highway in Inner Mongolia are two gigantic Apatosaurus, stretching to kiss each other. Many dinosaur fossils have been found in this area.

Transformational
Beijing, China
Standing a mighty 10 m (33 ft) tall, and made of wrecked cars and scrap metal, this statue of Optimus Prime from the *Transformers* films stands near Beijing's Olympic Park.

What a big baby!
Visakhapatnam, India
There are many statues along the beach in Visakhapatnam, including this one of a giant baby 3.5 m (11½ ft) tall.

Strange sculptures

Not all sculptures are exhibited in museums and galleries, many are found in streets and squares around the world. Some of these can be quite bizarre.

Headstand
Melbourne, Australia
This statue of Charles La Trobe outside La Trobe University turns learning on its head.

TURKEY, SO THAT THEY COULD BE PHOTOGRAPHED FROM SPACE.

Hydraulophone
Canada
Each jet on this watery keyboard produces a sound when covered by the fingers.

Ugly stick
Newfoundland, Canada
Typically fashioned out of a mop, bells, and tin cans, the player shakes the stick to produce a percussive sound.

Ice instruments
Norway, Sweden
These cold creations are made every year for a concert, chainsawed into their final shape just moments before the performance.

Alphorn *Switzerland*
This enormous traditional horn was used to call cows in from their pastures for milking.

Udderbot *USA*
A hybrid of a bottle and a rubber glove, this odd instrument is played by blowing across the top of the bottle and squeezing the glove's water-filled fingers to alter the sound.

Chrysalis
USA
With its circular shape inspired by the famous calendars of the ancient Aztecs, this acoustic instrument was designed to sound like the wind.

Mouthbow *Africa*
These ancient bows are plucked with the hand while one end is held in the mouth, to create resonance (deep sound).

Cajón
Peru
This is simply a wooden box with a hole – used as a percussion instrument.

Offbeat instruments

From the old to the new, musicians around the world have created many extraordinary instruments. The strange sounds they make may not be music to your ears, but these instruments are sure to find an audience somewhere.

Musical mammals
The animals of the Thai Elephant Orchestra use their trunks to play a wide range of percussion instruments. They have even released several albums.

SOME SAND DUNES SING! THE DEEP HUMMING NOISE IS MADE WHEN SAND

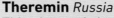

Treshchotka
Russia
These wooden clappers are popular in Russian folk music.

Theremin *Russia*
This electronic instrument can be played without even touching it. If you hover your hands over the antennae, it produces eerie noises, like those used in spooky films.

Musical spoons *Russia*
Although they might be mistaken for ordinary cookware, these colourful spoons are made of a harder wood and are used to make rhythmical music.

Yaybahar *Turkey*
A combination of a string instrument and a percussion instrument, the yaybahar can be played in several different ways to produce sounds.

Kaisatsuko
Japan
Played by turning a small handle and fingering the two strings, this experimental instrument is similar to a fiddle.

Sheng
China
Usually made up of 17 bamboo pipes and a mouthpiece the player blows into, the sheng is one of the oldest Chinese instruments. Examples of it date back to 1100 BCE.

Mbira
Southern and Eastern Africa
This ancient African instrument has metal prongs, which create different notes when plucked.

Nose flute
The Philippines
This flute is played by blowing air through the nose rather than through the mouth.

The Vegetable Orchestra
This orchestra from Austria crafts its instruments from fresh vegetables. However, their concerts are not just designed to appeal to the ears. At the end of the performance, the audience is also served freshly made vegetable soup.

Wire fence
Australia
Musician Jon Rose uses a bow to play an unlikely instrument – the wire fence. He has displayed his talents on many different fences worldwide.

GRAINS RUB AGAINST EACH OTHER AS THEY SLIDE DOWN THE DUNE.

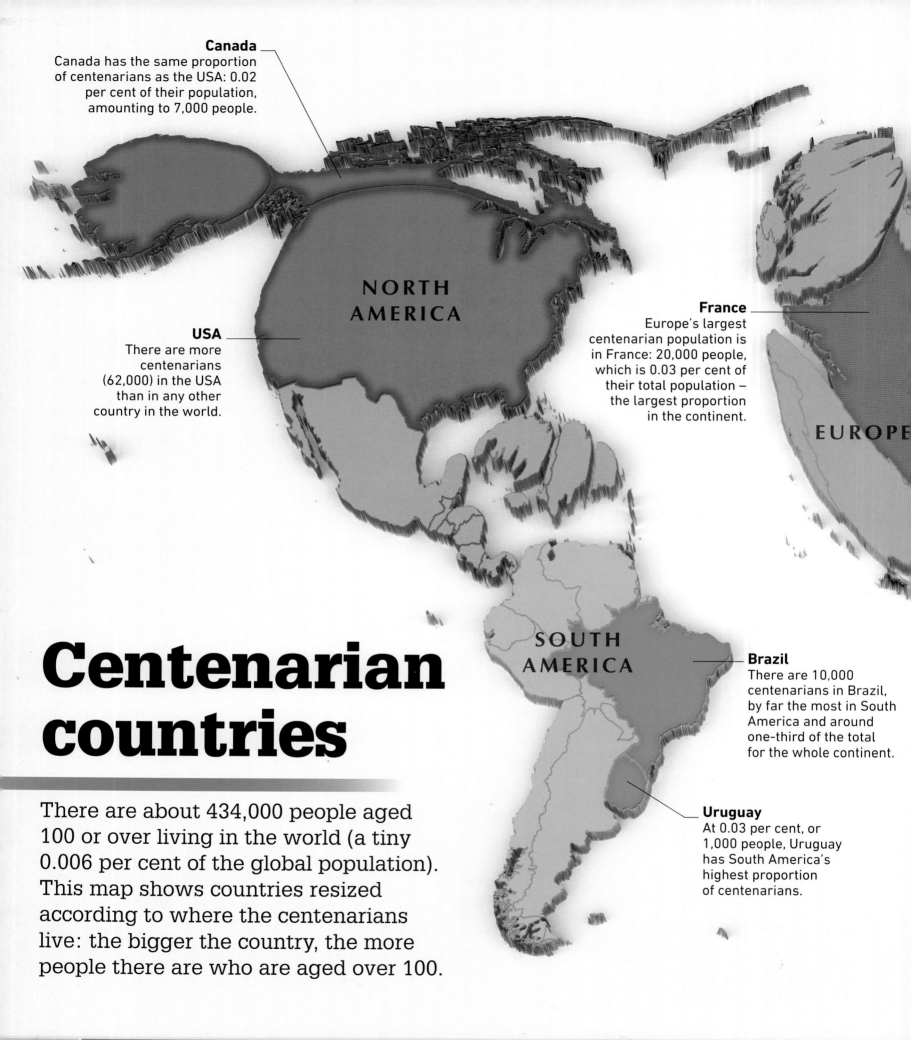

Canada
Canada has the same proportion of centenarians as the USA: 0.02 per cent of their population, amounting to 7,000 people.

NORTH AMERICA

USA
There are more centenarians (62,000) in the USA than in any other country in the world.

France
Europe's largest centenarian population is in France: 20,000 people, which is 0.03 per cent of their total population – the largest proportion in the continent.

EUROPE

Centenarian countries

SOUTH AMERICA

Brazil
There are 10,000 centenarians in Brazil, by far the most in South America and around one-third of the total for the whole continent.

Uruguay
At 0.03 per cent, or 1,000 people, Uruguay has South America's highest proportion of centenarians.

There are about 434,000 people aged 100 or over living in the world (a tiny 0.006 per cent of the global population). This map shows countries resized according to where the centenarians live: the bigger the country, the more people there are who are aged over 100.

ONLY 16 PER CENT OF THE WORLD'S POPULATION LIVES IN HIGH-INCOME

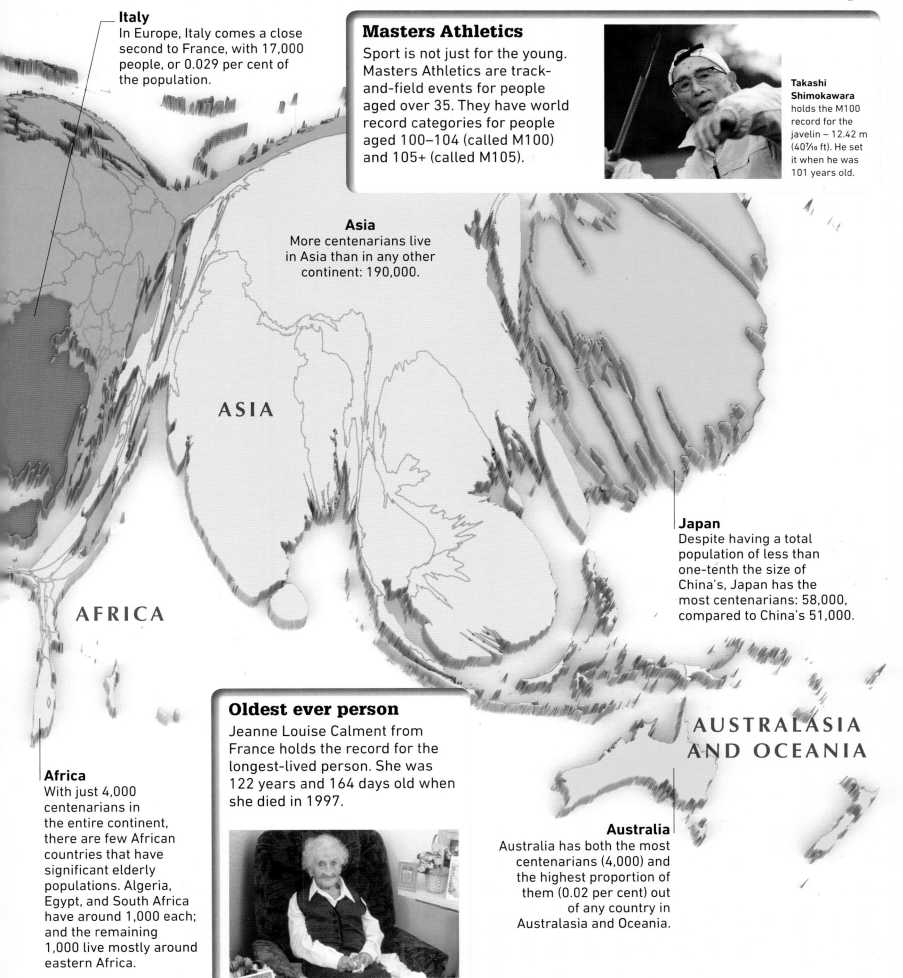

Italy
In Europe, Italy comes a close second to France, with 17,000 people, or 0.029 per cent of the population.

Masters Athletics
Sport is not just for the young. Masters Athletics are track-and-field events for people aged over 35. They have world record categories for people aged 100–104 (called M100) and 105+ (called M105).

Takashi Shimokawara holds the M100 record for the javelin – 12.42 m (40⁷⁄₁₀ ft). He set it when he was 101 years old.

Asia
More centenarians live in Asia than in any other continent: 190,000.

ASIA

Japan
Despite having a total population of less than one-tenth the size of China's, Japan has the most centenarians: 58,000, compared to China's 51,000.

AFRICA

Africa
With just 4,000 centenarians in the entire continent, there are few African countries that have significant elderly populations. Algeria, Egypt, and South Africa have around 1,000 each; and the remaining 1,000 live mostly around eastern Africa.

Oldest ever person
Jeanne Louise Calment from France holds the record for the longest-lived person. She was 122 years and 164 days old when she died in 1997.

AUSTRALASIA AND OCEANIA

Australia
Australia has both the most centenarians (4,000) and the highest proportion of them (0.02 per cent) out of any country in Australasia and Oceania.

History

Abandoned Alaska

Not all history is in the ancient past. There are hundreds of towns like Kennecott, Alaska, USA, which thrived during the mining boom but were abandoned less than 100 years ago.

Callanish Stones
Isle of Lewis, Scotland
A cross-shaped site from about 3000 BCE.

Newgrange
County Meath, Ireland
This large burial ground, known as a passage chamber, was built around 3200 BCE.

Drombeg Stone Circle
County Cork, Ireland
This Bronze Age stone circle is about 2,000 years old.

Seahenge
Norfolk, England
Discovered on a beach, this circle of oak trunks is about 4,000 years old.

Dolmen of Menga
Andalusia, Spa[...]
Built in the thir[...] millenium BCE, th[...] 25-m (82-ft) long[...] burial chamber i[...] one of Europe[...] largest megalithic structures.

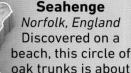

Carnac Stones
Brittany, France

Blythe Intaglios
California, USA
Giant human and animal pictures at this site have been drawn on the desert floor. They could be as much as 2,000 years old.

Olmec Heads
Mexico
These colossal stone heads were carved by the Olmecs, the first great civilization of Mexico.

Stonehenge
Wiltshire, England
Built about 5,000 years ago, this is one of the most famous megalithic sites in the world.

Uffington White Horse
Oxfordshire, England
A 110-m (360-ft) horse is carved into the hillside. It is thought to be at least 3,000 years old.

Taulas of Menorca
Balearic Islands, Spain
These megaliths were erected 3000–1000 BCE for unknown purposes.

📍 **Geoglyphs**

Geoglyphs are one of the most ancient artforms. These huge pictures carved into the landscape include images of people and animals, but many are unexplained shapes.

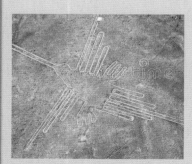

Nazca Lines Around 370 geoglyphs – including a 93-m (305-ft) long hummingbird – have been discovered in the Nazca Desert, Peru.

Paracas Candelabra
Pisco, Peru
This mysterious geoglyph is 183 m (600 ft) long and is located on a coastal hill.

Sun Stones
Brazil
Hundreds of these stone structures have been discovered in the Amazon rainforest.

Stone Circles of Senegambia
The Gambia and Senegal
Groups of stone circles in a sacred site extend along the River Gambia.

Atacama Giant
Huara, Northern Chile
This vast god figure was cut into the ground, is 119 m (390 ft) long, and is thought to be about 1,000 years old.

Some **stone circles** may have been used for **studying** the **night skies**.

THE BUILDERS OF STONEHENGE IN ENGLAND HAULED SOME OF THE

Megaliths

Some of the oldest manmade structures on Earth are prehistoric monuments constructed with massive stones called megaliths. At various sites around the world, megaliths can be seen standing in circles or rows, or used in tomb buildings.

Carnac Stones The world's largest group of standing stones can be found in Brittany, France. There are nearly 3,000 stones set in rows, some of which may date to 4500 BCE.

Caucasian Dolmens
Caucasus, Russia
Some 3,000 monuments, built using precisely cut stone blocks, are dotted throughout the Caucasian mountain range.

Longyou Caves
Zhejiang Province, China
Enormous, manmade caverns, decorated with wall carvings, have been carved out of the sandstone hills.

Gangwha Dolmens
South Korea
This area is home to roughly 120 stone tombs that date to the first millennium BCE.

Lore Lindu
Sulawesi, Indonesia
This Indonesian island is home to over 400 granite megaliths, some of which represent human forms.

Megaliths
Bouar, Central African Republic
More than 70 groups of stone settings dating to the first millennium BCE have been found in the area surrounding this central African city.

Unfinished Obelisk
Aswan, Egypt
Located in a quarry, this is the tallest obelisk (stone pillar) ever found. It would have stood a mighty 42 m (138 ft) high.

Dolmens of Kerala *India*
Hundreds of stone burial chambers have been found in this area. They could be more than 2,000 years old.

Mega monuments

Builders in the prehistoric world had primitive equipment but amazing engineering skills and big ideas. They made gigantic stone monuments and land drawings that have lasted for thousands of years and even influenced modern artists.

Marree Man
South Australia
This 4-km (2½-mile) long drawing of a man with a spear was marked out on the ground around 1998.

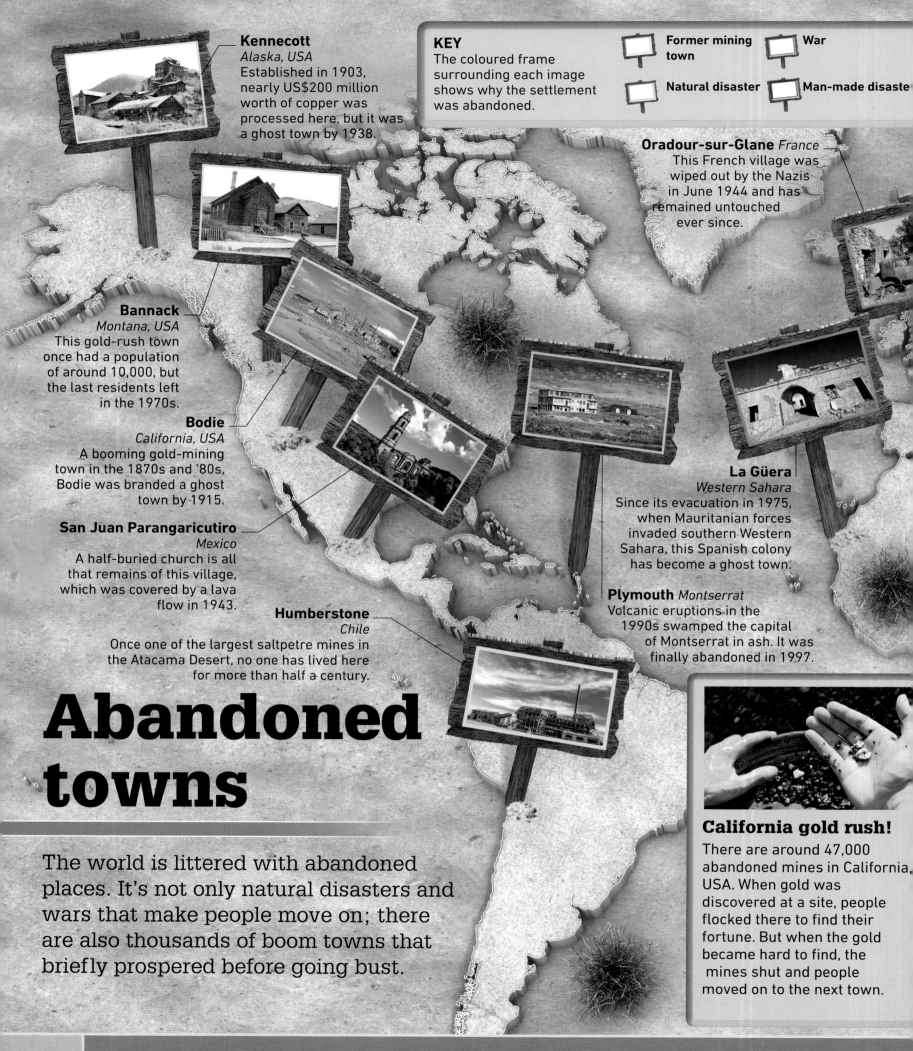

Kennecott
Alaska, USA
Established in 1903, nearly US$200 million worth of copper was processed here, but it was a ghost town by 1938.

Oradour-sur-Glane *France*
This French village was wiped out by the Nazis in June 1944 and has remained untouched ever since.

Bannack
Montana, USA
This gold-rush town once had a population of around 10,000, but the last residents left in the 1970s.

Bodie
California, USA
A booming gold-mining town in the 1870s and '80s, Bodie was branded a ghost town by 1915.

San Juan Parangaricutiro
Mexico
A half-buried church is all that remains of this village, which was covered by a lava flow in 1943.

Humberstone
Chile
Once one of the largest saltpetre mines in the Atacama Desert, no one has lived here for more than half a century.

La Güera
Western Sahara
Since its evacuation in 1975, when Mauritanian forces invaded southern Western Sahara, this Spanish colony has become a ghost town.

Plymouth *Montserrat*
Volcanic eruptions in the 1990s swamped the capital of Montserrat in ash. It was finally abandoned in 1997.

Abandoned towns

The world is littered with abandoned places. It's not only natural disasters and wars that make people move on; there are also thousands of boom towns that briefly prospered before going bust.

California gold rush!
There are around 47,000 abandoned mines in California, USA. When gold was discovered at a site, people flocked there to find their fortune. But when the gold became hard to find, the mines shut and people moved on to the next town.

Pripyat *Ukraine*
Following the disaster at Chernobyl's nuclear power station in 1986, this city was declared radioactively dangerous for humans for at least 24,000 years.

Kadykchan
Magadan Oblast, Russia
Built by prisoners in World War II, this coal-mining town was officially empty by 2010.

Hashima Island
Japan
Known for its underwater coal mines, residents left this island when the mines shut in 1974.

Agdam
Azerbaijan
Captured by Armenian forces in July 1993, every one of this town's 40,000 residents fled and never came back.

Nagoro
Japan

Craco
Italy
A series of earthquakes and landslides have made this southern Italian hill town inhabitable.

Bokor Hill Station
Cambodia
This luxury resort and retreat for French colonial residents was abandoned in the 1970s due to war.

Dallol
Ethiopia
Once a busy mining town, the settlement here – in one of the hottest and remotest places on Earth – was abandoned in the 1950s.

Dhanushkodi
India
This town was destroyed during a cyclone in 1964 and was never rebuilt.

Wittenoom *Australia*
The site of Australia's only blue asbestos mine, the residents moved on when the mine was shut in 1966.

Kolmanskop
Namibia
Diamonds were first discovered here in 1908, but the town was abandoned by 1956.

◉ Village of dolls

The village of Nagoro in Japan is one of many villages around the world whose population is in decline. Here, when one of the villagers dies, a life-sized doll is made to replace them.

GHOST TOWN IN THE WORLD THAT IS STILL THE CAPITAL OF A COUNTRY.

127

Pig War 1859
San Juan Islands, USA
A rogue British pig eating an American's potatoes kicked off this short-lived border dispute.

War of Pork and Beans 1838–39 *Maine, USA*
Casualties were avoided in this territorial dispute allegedly named for the rations of the soldiers stationed there.

Three Hundred and Thirty-Five Years War
The Netherlands and Isles of Scilly, UK
This "war that wasn't" pitted the Dutch against an English Civil War faction who had retreated to the Scilly Isles. No shots were fired, but an official peace treaty was only signed in 1986.

Pastry War 1838–39
Mexico
This conflict arose when a French pastry chef's bakery was looted. When Mexico refused to pay compensation, the French government went to war.

War of Jenkins' Ear 1739–42
The Caribbean
When British captain Robert Jenkins claimed the Spanish coastguard had cut off his ear, the two countries' subsequent skirmishes eventually led to the War of Austrian Succession.

Football War 1969
Honduras
A tense World Cup qualifying match between El Salvador and Honduras was one of several factors that caused hostility between the two nations. El Salvador launched an invasion just 18 days later.

Weird wars

Warfare may not strike you as weird, but were these crazy causes really worth fighting for? Many barmy battles throughout history began for the strangest of reasons, or ended up being carried out in curious circumstances.

No **people** were **harmed** in the **Pig War** – but the pig was **shot**

The "Rotabuggy"
War can bring about some odd inventions. During World War II, the British Army experimented with a flying jeep, called the Rotabuggy. It was designed to deliver the jeep to the battlefield.

Battle of Otryae 74 BCE
Modern-day Turkey
During the Third Mithridatic War, Roman general Lucullus was sent to invade the kingdom of Pontus, but both armies fled the battlefield at the sight of a fiery meteorite falling from the sky.

Battle of Texel 1795 *The Netherlands*
French cavalry galloped across the ice to fight against warships when a Dutch fleet became trapped in frozen waters.

Stray Dog War 1925
Bulgaria
Crossing into Bulgaria to retrieve his runaway dog, a Greek soldier was shot, triggering a war that led to more than 50 deaths. The fate of the dog is unknown.

War of the Oaken Bucket 1325
Northern Italy
When the city-state of Modena stole a bucketful of booty from nearby Bologna, the proud Bolognese sent their army to recover it.

Siege of Halicarnassus 334 BCE
Present-day Turkey
This raid was launched when two drunk soldiers had a fight over who was the bravest, and so scaled the city walls themselves.

Anglo-Zanzibar War 1896
Zanzibar, Tanzania
Considered the shortest-ever war, this clash came about when the British ordered a Sultan to give up his throne. He refused, the British destroyed the palace, and the war was over just 40 minutes after it had begun.

Emu War 1932
Western Australia
Emus became the enemy in this bizarre battle between birds and humans. When the emus started destroying crops, humans took up arms, but only managed to kill fewer than 1,000. The emus eventually left of their own accord.

BUT CAME BACK WITH 81, HAVING PICKED UP A FRIEND.

Bombast
Europe, 16th century
Men used this secret stuffing made of horsehair, wool, or sawdust to pad out their shoulders, stiffen sleeves, and create bulging breeches.

Liripipe
Europe, medieval period
This trailing tube of cloth hanging from the back of a hood could reach over 1 m (3 ft) in length.

Crackowes
Europe, 14th and 15th centuries
These shoes are named for the Polish city Kraków, where they came from. Some had toes so long they had to be attached to the knees by chains.

White face paint
England, 16th century
Women in the Elizabethan era copied the queen's pale complexion by wearing make-up made of deadly white lead paste.

Bliauts
Europe, 12th century
These impractical gowns with flowing sleeves often contained hundreds of folds and pleats.

Plucked eyelashes
Europe, 15th century
Foreheads were in fashion in the 1400s, so women removed their eyebrows and eyelashes to emphasize them.

Chopines
Venice, Italy, 16th century
These stately slippers kept noble women's dresses clear of the dirt in wet, muddy streets.

Panniers
Europe, 18th century
Huge hoops under dresses made a woman's skirt so wide that she could not fit through doorways.

Chemise à la Reine
France, 18th century
This simple dress worn by Queen Marie Antoinette shocked the public, as it looked like a commoner's undershirt, not a dress worn by a queen.

Spanish fashion
Europe, 16th century
Many countries copied influential Spanish fashions, including capes, corsets, ruffs, and traditional waistcoats.

Hair-raising wigs
Towering wigs became the height of fashion in the 17th and 18th centuries. Often scented, powdered, and covered with jewels, these hairpieces could be up to 1.2 m (4 ft) high, and were made of human hair obtained from peasants or prisoners.

SOME ANCIENT BEAUTY REGIMES USED AN UNLIKELY INGREDIENT

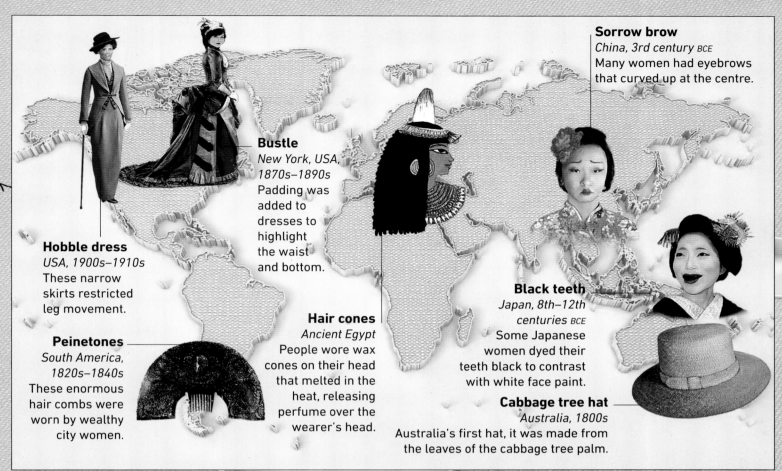

Sorrow brow
China, 3rd century BCE
Many women had eyebrows that curved up at the centre.

Bustle
New York, USA, 1870s–1890s
Padding was added to dresses to highlight the waist and bottom.

Hobble dress
USA, 1900s–1910s
These narrow skirts restricted leg movement.

Peinetones
South America, 1820s–1840s
These enormous hair combs were worn by wealthy city women.

Hair cones
Ancient Egypt
People wore wax cones on their head that melted in the heat, releasing perfume over the wearer's head.

Black teeth
Japan, 8th–12th centuries BCE
Some Japanese women dyed their teeth black to contrast with white face paint.

Cabbage tree hat
Australia, 1800s
Australia's first hat, it was made from the leaves of the cabbage tree palm.

Macaroni fashion
Europe, 18th century
Young British aristocrats often copied excessive Italian fashions. Those who did so were called "Macaronis".

European women did not start **wearing knickers** until the **19th** century.

Unibrow
Ancient Greece and Rome
Joined brows were considered a sign of purity. They could be faked by applying false hairs from goats.

Bygone beauty

Throughout history, the appearance of our ancestors has ranged from flamboyant to bizarre, and many of the products they used were deadly. These old-time fashion and beauty trends are a far cry from those you would find in a magazine today.

DUNG. THE ROMANS USED CROCODILE DUNG TO LIGHTEN THEIR FACES.

Healthy hair
UK, 1654
One 17th-century English medical manual suggested using chicken droppings as a cure for baldness.

Ketchup
USA, 1830s
This fun food was originally marketed as a medicine – said to cure anything from diarrhoea to indigestion – due to the vitamins in the tomatoes.

Powder of sympathy
Europe, 17th century
It was thought that applying this magical remedy to a weapon would help heal the wound it had caused.

Teething trouble
USA, 1849–1930s
Some infants never woke up again after taking Mrs Winslow's Soothing Syrup, a cure for teething babies. It contained both alcohol and the powerful drug morphine.

Toilet practice
USA, 1600s–1800s
The first colonists to arrive in America used dried corn cobs to keep clean. These were a lot softer than some of the other options, as many settlers used shells!

Trepanation
Worldwide, from 7000 BCE
Drilling a hole straight into the skull was a popular procedure in prehistoric times. It is thought to have been done to relieve pressure in the brain.

Native healing
South America
Folk healers called *curanderos* used chants and herbs to cure people in ancient Inca times.

In the **19th century**, a Prussian surgeon tried **chopping off** part of **the tongue** to cure stuttering.

Leeching
These bloodsucking creatures have been used as a gory cure for more than 2,500 years, and were thought to remove bad blood from the body. They are still used in some forms of surgery today.

MANY ANCIENT ROMAN PHYSICIANS WERE ALSO POISONERS WHO

Healing chants
Scandinavia, 700–1000 CE
The Vikings believed in the power of Norse letters, called runes, and used chants and charms to bring them good health.

Eating dirt
Europe, 500 BCE–19th century
Discs of clay from the Greek island of Lemnos used to be eaten as a remedy for many ills. They were stamped with a seal of approval and then distributed across Europe.

Quest for immortality
China, 259–210 BCE
Chinese emperor Qin Shi Huangdi desperately tried to avoid death by drinking tonics filled with mercury – a poisonous substance that probably caused his early demise.

Urine therapy
India, from ancient times
Ancient Indian religious texts describe the health benefits of drinking your own urine.

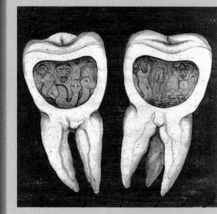

Tooth worms
Before modern-day dentists understood the reasons behind tooth decay, people used to believe that tiny worms living inside the teeth were responsible for dental problems. They attributed any tooth pain to the worm wiggling around.

Vile bile
Ancient China
In traditional Chinese medicine, elephant bile was gargled to get rid of bad breath, and was also believed to help improve eyesight.

Unusual ointments
Ancient Egypt
Ointments made from all kinds of animal dung were one of the staple cures in Egyptian society.

Mummy medicine
Arabian Peninsula, Europe, 16th–18th centuries
The ground-up remains of Egyptian mummies were once a trendy ingredient to put into medicinal potions and ointments.

Historical health

Rheumatism cure
Australia, 19th century
One man's experience in the town of Eden led to claims that climbing inside a whale carcass would relieve joint pain.

Doctors of the past could actually be more of a hindrance to your health than a help. Some of their crazy cures ranged from the unhygienic to the downright dodgy and dangerous.

Maine penny
Maine, USA
The discovery of this Norse coin from 1065–1080 CE could prove that the Vikings reached Maine 500 years before Christopher Columbus arrived in the Americas.

Mystery stone
New Hampshire, USA
This is an unusual stone carved with ancient symbols. Its age, purpose, and origin are unknown.

Roman dodecahedron
Across Europe
About 100 small, 12-sided shapes have been unearthed. What the Romans used them for is a mystery.

Tecaxic-Calixtlahuaca head
Mexico
Discovered in 1933, this terracotta head appears to be of Roman origin. How it ended up buried among Aztec artefacts from the 15th and early 16th centuries is mysterious.

Quimbaya figurines
Colombia
A collection of small, gold figurines, from 300–1000 CE, depict flying animals, birds, and insects. Some people have said they also show ancient flying machines.

Diquís spheres
Costa Rica
These large, spherical stones are scattered across Costa Rica. No one knows how they were made or what they were made for.

Voynich manuscript
In 1912, a Polish bookseller bought a 15th-century text containing illustrations of herbs and astrological charts, though no one could decipher the writing. It may be written in code or in an invented language, or it may be a hoax, but despite a great deal of study the text has remained a mystery.

Rongorongo text
Easter Island, Chile
These pieces of wood dating back to the early 17th century are carved with an early form of writing. So far, analysts have failed to decipher the script.

Saksaywaman wall
Cusco, Peru
Walls around the Inca fortress at Cusco are made of stones cut and fitted together leaving virtually no gaps. The method used to create such a perfect fit is a puzzle.

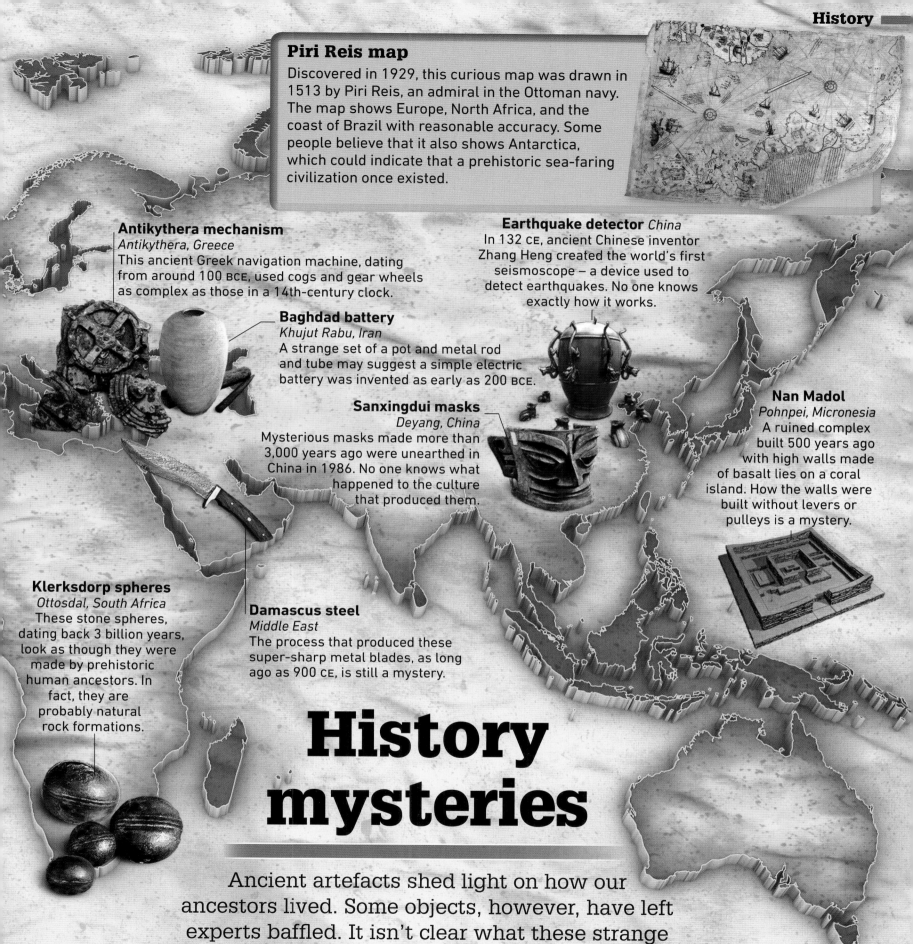

Piri Reis map
Discovered in 1929, this curious map was drawn in 1513 by Piri Reis, an admiral in the Ottoman navy. The map shows Europe, North Africa, and the coast of Brazil with reasonable accuracy. Some people believe that it also shows Antarctica, which could indicate that a prehistoric sea-faring civilization once existed.

Antikythera mechanism
Antikythera, Greece
This ancient Greek navigation machine, dating from around 100 BCE, used cogs and gear wheels as complex as those in a 14th-century clock.

Earthquake detector *China*
In 132 CE, ancient Chinese inventor Zhang Heng created the world's first seismoscope – a device used to detect earthquakes. No one knows exactly how it works.

Baghdad battery
Khujut Rabu, Iran
A strange set of a pot and metal rod and tube may suggest a simple electric battery was invented as early as 200 BCE.

Sanxingdui masks
Deyang, China
Mysterious masks made more than 3,000 years ago were unearthed in China in 1986. No one knows what happened to the culture that produced them.

Nan Madol
Pohnpei, Micronesia
A ruined complex built 500 years ago with high walls made of basalt lies on a coral island. How the walls were built without levers or pulleys is a mystery.

Klerksdorp spheres
Ottosdal, South Africa
These stone spheres, dating back 3 billion years, look as though they were made by prehistoric human ancestors. In fact, they are probably natural rock formations.

Damascus steel
Middle East
The process that produced these super-sharp metal blades, as long ago as 900 CE, is still a mystery.

History mysteries

Ancient artefacts shed light on how our ancestors lived. Some objects, however, have left experts baffled. It isn't clear what these strange items were for, or how our ancient ancestors managed to produce them.

Fun facts

Between two continents
Iceland lies across two continental plates, and people can dive right between them in the Silfra – a rift, or crack, in southwest Iceland where the North American and Eurasian tectonic plates meet.

North and Central America

Canada is home to **two-thirds** of all the **polar bears** in the world.

Half and half

The Haskell Free Library and Opera House is half in Canada and half in the USA. The opera house stage is in Rock Island, Quebec, while most of the seats are in Derby Line, Vermont.

In **New York, USA,** you can hear more than **800 languages** being spoken.

The **most common** road name in the **USA** is **Second Street.** First Street is **third!**

New York, USA

In **Grand Central Station, New York,** all the departure boards display the wrong time – they say the train leaves **one minute** before it actually does, to stop people rushing for their train.

There is **15 times** as much snowfall in New York, USA, than there is at the South Pole each year. This is because the South Pole is a **cold desert** and receives very little precipitation.

It is illegal to sell a haunted house in **New York, USA,** without warning the buyer.

More than 40 buildings in **Manhattan, New York, USA,** including the Chrysler Building (right), are so large, they have their own zip code (post code).

10017 ZIP CODE

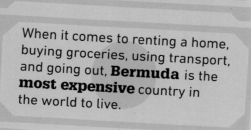

When it comes to renting a home, buying groceries, using transport, and going out, **Bermuda** is the **most expensive** country in the world to live.

The USA is home to **546 billionaires**, more than any other country in the world: **103** of them live in **New York**!

The **glasses** on the statue of **John Lennon** in the John Lennon Park in **Havana, Cuba,** have been stolen so often that a security guard holds them and puts them on the statue if visitors ask.

Mexico's **Great Pyramid of Cholula** is the **biggest pyramid in the world**. Its base is 400 sq m (1,300 sq ft), making it four times the size of the Great Pyramid of Giza (although at 55 m (180 ft) tall, it's less than half Giza's height).

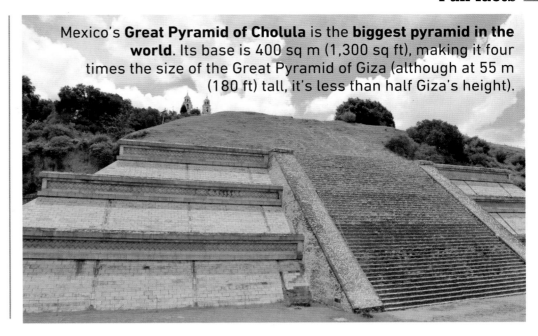

The Panama Canal has a toll based on weight. In 1928, American **Richard Halliburton** paid 36 cents to swim through the canal; while in 2016, the container ship **MOL *Benefactor*** had to pay nearly **$1 million.**

The USA has **15,095** airports – more than any other country in the world.

Jamaica has **1,600 churches** – more **per sq km (sq mile)** than any other country.

Divers at the **Roatan National Park** in Honduras have tried to train Caribbean reef sharks to eat lionfish – an invasive species that is damaging the reef ecosystem.

Until **2014,** there were no street names or house numbers in **Costa Rica**. Post was addressed using **landmarks** and **directions** instead.

South America

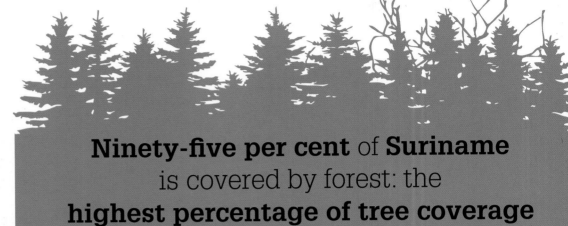

Colombia's national sport, **Tejo**, involves throwing a **metal puck (disc)** into a target that contains packets of **gunpowder!**

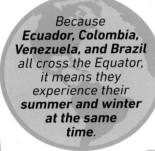

Ninety-five per cent of **Suriname** is covered by forest: the **highest percentage of tree coverage** of any country in the world.

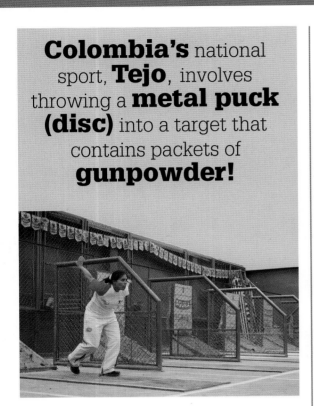

*Because **Ecuador, Colombia, Venezuela,** and **Brazil** all cross the Equator, it means they experience their **summer and winter at the same time.***

La Paz – the capital of Bolivia – *was the first city in South America to get electricity. It was fuelled not by coal or gas, but by llama dung.*

Paraguay's flag is the only country flag to have **two different sides.** The nation's coat of arms is on the front and the **Treasury Seal** and **motto ("Peace and Justice")** is on the back.

Uruguay has no official religion. Instead of Christmas, it has **Family Day**; other holidays include **Tourism Week** and **Beach Day**.

Guyana is the only **South American** nation that has **English** as its official language.

Venezuela is named after **Venice, Italy,** because the country reminded European explorers of the **Italian city.**

Ecuador – named after the Equator – is the only country named after a geographic feature. **The town of Ciudad Mitad del Mundo** has a painted Equator line where people can stand in **both hemispheres** at the same time… except it's **240 m (787 ft) south** of where the Equator is said to actually fall.

The **plants** of the Amazon rainforest produce more than **20 per cent** of the world's oxygen.

It's thought that **scientists** have yet to study around **90 per cent** of the plants in the Amazon rainforest.

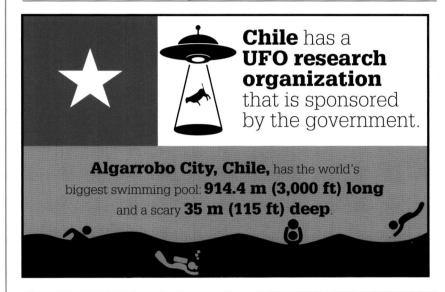

Chile has a **UFO research organization** that is sponsored by the government.

Algarrobo City, Chile, has the world's biggest swimming pool: **914.4 m (3,000 ft) long** and a scary **35 m (115 ft) deep**.

The **Amazon River** pumps so much water into the **Atlantic**, fresh water can be found more than **160 km (100 miles)** out to sea.

More species of fish can be found in the Amazon River than in the whole of the Atlantic Ocean.

Amazon River dolphins are pink.

In 1892, **Argentina** became the **first country** in the world to use **fingerprints** to **convict a criminal**.

Almost half of all South American people live in **Brazil**.

Brazil has a border with every South American country except **Ecuador** and **Chile**.

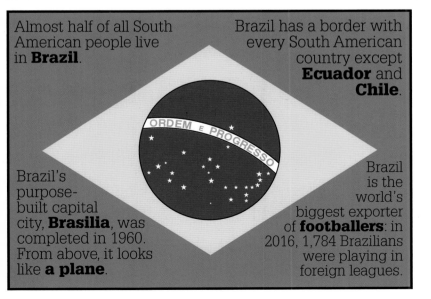

Brazil's purpose-built capital city, **Brasilia**, was completed in 1960. From above, it looks like **a plane**.

Brazil is the world's biggest exporter of **footballers**: in 2016, 1,784 Brazilians were playing in foreign leagues.

There are more than **3,000 varieties** of potato and **55 varieties** of **corn** grown in Peru. Corn colours include **black**, white, and **purple** (and yellow).

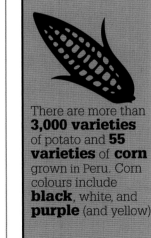

Yellow underwear is a traditional New Year's gift in Peru. It is meant to bring **good luck!**

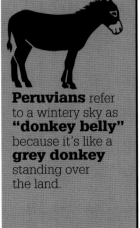

Peruvians refer to a wintery sky as **"donkey belly"** because it's like a **grey donkey** standing over the land.

Africa

The Atlas Film Studios in Morocco are the largest film studios in the world.

Somalia has the world's biggest population of camels – around **7.2 million animals.**

Togo has only ever won **one** Olympic medal: a **2008 bronze** in **kayaking**, won by a man who'd only ever visited Togo once.

Nigeria has the **world's second-largest film industry**, after **India.** Around **50 films** are produced per week in **"Nollywood"**.

Namibia's Skeleton Coast, where the Namib Desert meets the sea, has such thick fog that it's known as the "shore of a thousand shipwrecks".

Half of all the gold in the world comes from one location: **Witwatersrand, South Africa**.

The **Ghanian** currency, **cedi,** is named after the **cowrie (sea) shells** that used to be used as money.

In Botswana, the currency is pula, which means **"rain"** – rain is very scarce, and therefore prized. Pula is made up of thebes, which means **"shield"**.

There are about **2,000 pyramids** in northern **Sudan** – about twice the amount in **Egypt**. The oldest is **4,600 years old**.

Ethiopia uses a **different calendar system** to the rest of the world. As a result, an Ethiopian year consists of **13 months** rather than 12.

Coffee is **Kenya's** main export – but Kenyans prefer to **drink tea**.

If **dung beetles** left the **African plains**, it would take just **a month** for the land to be **waist-high in poo**.

Around **90 per cent** of **species** found on **Madagascar** are **unique** to the island.

The world record for the **highest-altitude pizza delivery** on land was set at the top of **Mt Kilimanjaro**. It took **four days** to deliver the pizza **745 km (463 miles)** from the restaurant in **Tanzania** to the peak **5,897 m (19,347 ft)** up.

"B!g Rush" *in Durban, South Africa, is the world's tallest swing. The seat is 9 m (29½ ft) above the ground, and the crossbar sits another 88 m (289 ft) above that.*

Europe

There is a **golf course** on the **Finland-Sweden** border where **half the holes** are in Finland and **half** are in Sweden.

The **world's highest toilet** sits more than **4,200 m (13,780 ft)** above sea level at the top of **Mont Blanc, France.**

In **1879** in **Liège, Belgium,** the post office hired **37 cats** to deliver mail, **training them** using their "homing instincts". **It didn't work**.

In 133 BCE, **Rome** became the **first city** in the world to have a population of **one million people**.

Bratislava, the capital city of **Slovakia**, is the **only** capital city to **border other countries** – Austria and Hungary.

Bratislava

There's a **720-m (2,363-ft)** long **zip line** between **Spain** and **Portugal.**

The **bridges** on **euro banknotes** were deliberately designed **not** to look like **real bridges** so **no country** could claim them – until a **Dutch designer** decided to build bridges in **Rotterdam, The Netherlands,** to look like those on the money, even **copying the colours.**

It takes **one minute** to ride, but, because you cross a time zone, you also **travel back in time** by one hour.

In Armenia, the **school timetable** includes compulsory chess lessons.

The **Greek national anthem** is the longest in the world. It has **158 verses**.

The national animal of **Scotland** is the **unicorn**.

It's **illegal** to **own** a **pet lizard, snake, or turtle** in **Iceland**.

In Germany, the **Chancellery building** is known as the **Bundeswaschmaschine ("federal washing machine")** because its **square** shape and **round windows** make it look like a washing machine

Every year since **1990**, the town of **Pelhrimov** in the **Czech Republic** holds a **festival** where they try to **break** as many **wacky world records** as possible, including **racing up ladders** and balancing a **car on salt cellars.**

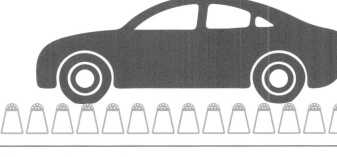

The **Gyermekvasút Railway** in **Hungary** is run by **schoolchildren** aged **10** to **14**. From **selling tickets** to **acting as train conductors** and **operating the points**, they do everything except drive the trains. **(Train drivers are adults.)**

Lake Baikal, in Russia, is **so deep**, it holds **20 per cent** of the **world's** unfrozen fresh water.

 In several **European** countries, the @ **symbol** is named after **animals:**

 **Netherlands:** Monkey's tail

 Denmark/Sweden: The elephant's trunk

 Greece: Duckling

 Hungary: Worm or maggot

 Italy: Snail

 Macedonia: Little monkey

 Poland: Monkey

145

Asia

A **traditional Tibetan** way of **measuring distance** was by how many **cups of tea** were **needed** for the **journey**.

The **Himalayas** formed **25 million years** after the **dinosaurs** became **extinct**.

When a woman in **Georgia** sliced through a **cable** in **2011**, **it cut off the Internet** in the whole of **Armenia**.

Nepal is the only country in the world **not** to have **a square** or **rectangular flag**.

The Lut Desert in **Iran** is so **hot**, even **bacteria die**. A glass of milk left in the desert **won't ever go off**.

China owns all the **giant pandas** in the world – even those in **zoos abroad**.

Although **the tulip** is the **Dutch national flower**, it actually comes from **Turkey**. The word "tulip" comes from the **Turkish word tülbent**, meaning "turban".

The world's **tallest building**, the **Burj Khalifa** in **Dubai**, has such **fast lifts** that you can see **the Sun** set at **ground level**, get the lift to the top, and watch it set a **second time** from **the roof**.

Andamanese (the language spoken in India's **Andaman Islands**) has only **two** words for **numbers:** one that means **"one"** and another that means **"more than one"**.

In **South Korea**, when a **baby is born**, he or she is considered to be **a year old.** Then they turn older on **1 January** as well, so **babies born on 31 December** could be **2 years old** when they are, in fact, just **2 days old**.

Israel is the only **country** to have revived a **"dead" language** as its **national tongue**. Until the **state** was established, **Hebrew** was used only in prayers and for studying.

The **Binh Chau Hot Springs**, in **Vietnam**, reach **82 °C (180 °F)** – hot enough to **boil an egg** in about **10 minutes**.

Vending machines in **Japan** don't just dispense **drinks** and **chocolate**. You can also buy **live lobsters**, flying fish soup, **bowls of hot ramen (noodles)**, eggs, **lettuce**, bananas, and **underwear**.

Since the **1970s in Japan**, there's been a tradition to go to **KFC on Christmas Day.** It's believed this started when **visitors** couldn't find a whole **chicken** or **turkey** to make their own **celebratory lunch.**

In **1973**, archaeologists discovered **2,000-year-old seeds** in a **jar** in Masada, Israel. They were planted in **2005** and the **date-palm tree** that grew was of a **species** that had been **extinct** for **1,800 years**.

Japan and **China** supply more than **50 per cent** of the **world's silk**, using the **cocoons** of **silkworms**. Each cocoon is made of a strand of silk around **915 m (3,000 ft)** long.

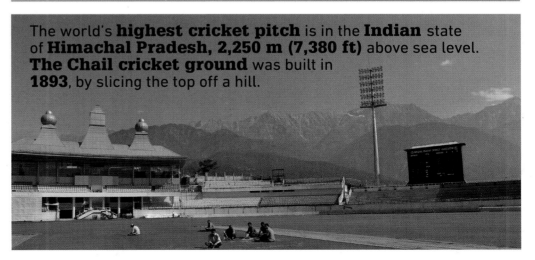

The world's **highest cricket pitch** is in the **Indian** state of **Himachal Pradesh, 2,250 m (7,380 ft)** above sea level. **The Chail cricket ground** was built in **1893**, by slicing the top off a hill.

Australasia and Oceania

The **Dingo Fence** in Australia is the **world's longest fence**. It runs **5,531 km** (3,437 miles) from **Jimbour, Queensland**, to the **Great Australian Bight, South Australia**.

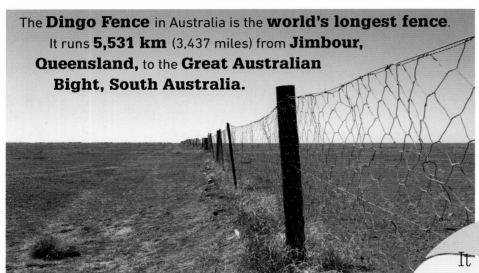

In **1940,** two planes from the Royal Australian Air Force **collided** in mid-air and got **stuck together.** Four crewmen bailed out, but **one remained** and made a safe landing.

Camels were introduced to **Australia** in **1840** as transport for **explorers** into the Outback. There are now **600,000–1 million wild camels** in Australia.

It would take more than **29 years** to see all of Australia's **10,685 beaches** if you visited **one a day.**

It is thought that Australia's population of **200 million crop-eating rabbits** is mainly the result of **one man**, who released **24 of them** into the wild **in 1859** for hunting.

Kangaroo Island, Australia, was named by the explorer **Matthew Flinders in 1802**, in gratitude for the **31 kangaroos** he and his crew turned into **soup.**

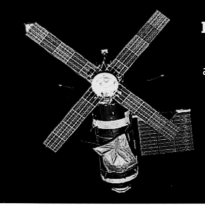

In 1979, the **US Skylab** space station burned up in **Earth's atmosphere** and large **chunks of debris** fell over Australia. The council of **Esperance, Western Australia,** "fined" NASA **$400 for littering.** (The fine was paid in **2009** by listeners of a **Californian radio station.**)

Ninety-mile Beach in the very north of New Zealand is actually 88 km (55 miles) long...

In Fiji, if you wear a **frangipani** flower tucked behind your **right ear**, it means you're **looking for love**. If you wear one over your **left ear** it means you're **already taken**.

Tuvalu is a **Tuvaluan word** meaning **"cluster of eight"**. There are **nine** islands in **Tuvalu!**

The origins of **bungee jumping** lie in **naghol** ("**land diving**") from **Pentecost Island, Vanuatu.** Men and boys jump off **bamboo towers 27 m (90 ft) tall,** using **vines** as their bungee rope. Only their **hair** is allowed to **touch the ground** on the dive, and if it **does,** then, according to legend, there will be a successful **yam harvest.**

There are more than **10,000 islands** in **Oceania**. Excluding **Australia,** they have a **total land area** of just **822,800 sq km** (317,700 sq miles), and so could all fit inside **Australia** more than **nine times.**

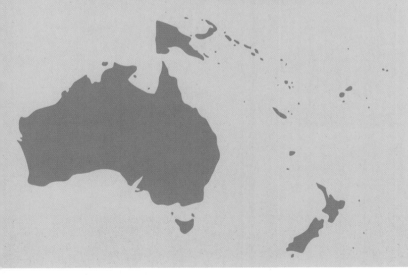

The **Royal New Zealand Air Force** has the country's national bird – **the kiwi** – as its logo. Kiwis are **flightless.**

There are **no snakes** in **New Zealand.**

30 December 2011 never existed for people in Samoa and Tokelau. These countries moved the **International Date Line** so they could be in the **same time zone** as **Australia** and **New Zealand**. As they hopped **"forwards"**, they lost a day.

When there are no **free seats** on **crowded buses** in **Samoa**, people invite others to **sit on their laps** – even if they're **strangers!**

149

What's in a name?

The world's longest place name is:

Krung Thep Mahanakhon Amon Rattanakosin Mahinthara Ayutthaya Mahadilok Phop Noppharat Ratchathani Burirom Udomratchaniwet Mahasathan Amon Piman Awatan Sathit Sakkathattiya Witsanukam Prasit

This means: "The city of angels, the great city, the residence of the Emerald Buddha, the impregnable city (of Ayutthaya) of God Indra, the grand capital of the world endowed with nine precious gems, the happy city, abounding in an enormous Royal Palace that resembles the heavenly abode where reigns the reincarnated god, a city given by Indra and built by Vishnukarn."

In **Thailand**, it's usually abbreviated to **Krung Thep ("City of Angels")** – but the rest of the world calls it **Bangkok.**

Singapore (**Singapura**) comes from the **Sanskrit** *Simhapuram,* meaning **"Lion City"**.

No one knows how *Sierra Leone* – Spanish for **"Lion Mountains"** – got its name. Some think it is because the country's mountains look like **sleeping lions** or **lions' teeth**. Others think it is because thunder in the mountains sounds like a **lion**.

Cameroon is named after the **Portuguese word** for shrimp: *camarões*.

There is a **town in Norway** called **Hell**. This doesn't **sound** appealing **in English**, but in **Norwegian**, it means **"success"**.

Spain (*España*) comes from the **Latin** *Hispana,* popularly thought to mean **"land of rabbits"**.

Panama may come from local words for **"place of many fish"** or **"many butterflies"**.

Brazil is named for the **nut-bearing tree – not** the other way around.

Don't go there!

These place names could really deter visitors...

- **Devil's Bit**
  County Tipperary, Ireland
- **Disappointment Island**
  New Zealand
- **Eek**
  Alaska, USA
- **Hongerige Wolf** (Hungry Wolf), Groningen, Netherlands
- **Pity Me**
  Durham, UK
- **Stupid Lake**
  Manitoba, Canada

... but these places sound great!

- **Batman**
  Turkey
- **Cool**
  California, USA
- **Desire**
  Pennsylvania, USA
- **Fairy Dell**
  Victoria, Australia
- **Goodenough Island**
  Papua New Guinea
- **Surprise**
  Arizona, USA

Where am I?

Nameless, Tennessee, USA
No Name, Colorado, USA
No Place, County Durham, UK
Nowhere, Oklahoma, USA
Nowhere Else, Tasmania, Australia
Point No Point, Washington, USA
Uncertain, Texas, USA
Why, Arizona, USA

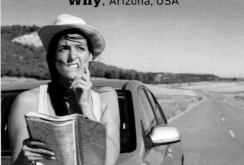

Head-Smashed-In Buffalo Jump, in Canada, is **named for** the ancient **practice** of **hunting bison** by forcing them to **stampede** over the **edge of a cliff** – something first done **12,000 years ago**.

SO GOOD THEY NAMED IT TWICE

 WATERFALL Eas Fors Waterfall, UK – means "waterfall waterfall waterfall" in Scottish Gaelic, Norse, and English.

 TOWN SQUARE Forumtorget, Sweden – means "the square square" in Latin and Swedish.

 VILLAGE Külaküla, Estonia – means "village village" in Estonian.

 COAST Côtes-d'Armor, France – means "coast of coast" in French and Breton.

 LAKE Järvijärvi, Finland – means "lake lake" in Finnish.

 TOWN Nyanza Lac, Burundi – means "lake lake" in Bantu and French... but this is a city, not a lake!

 MOUNTAIN Filefjell, Norway – means "mountain mountain" in Norwegian.

 ISLAND Isla Pulo, Philippines – means "island island" in Filipino.

LESS-CHEERFUL NAMES:
- **Boring**, Oregon, USA
- **Dull**, Perth and Kinross, UK
- **Bland Shire**, NSW, Australia

CHEERFUL NAMES:
- **Funny River** Alaska, USA
- **Ha! Ha! River** Quebec, Canada
- **Happy Adventure** Newfoundland, Canada
- **What Cheer** Iowa, USA

The world's longest single-word place name is:

Taumatawhakatangihangakoauauotamateaturipukakapikimaungahoronukupokaiwhenuakitanatahu

The Maori name of this New Zealand hill translates into: "The summit where Tamatea, the man with the big knees, the climber of mountains, the land-swallower who travelled about, played his nose flute to his loved one."

Global gestures

In **Albania**, Bulgaria, **Egypt**, Greece, **Iran**, Lebanon, **Sicily**, Syria, and Turkey, **nodding** the head **upwards once** means **"no"**.

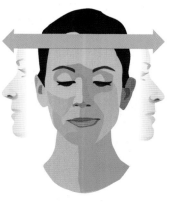

In **Bulgaria** and **southern Albania,** shaking your head from **side to side** means **"yes".**

In **India**, placing one's hands together is used as a **greeting** known as "**Namaste**".
In **Japan**, the same action is used to **ask for forgiveness** or to **say thank you**.

In **Nepal,** you **shake your hand** to say **no**.

If you wave the **back of your hand upwards** in **Australia,** Canada, **the UK,** and the USA, it means "go away". In Ghana, **India** the **Philippines**, and Vietnam, it means **"Come here!"**, because in these countries it is **rude** to beckon people with your palm held **upwards**.

Curling your finger to ask someone to "**come here**" is used in **Australia,** Canada, **the UK**, and the USA. In the **Philippines**, however, it is **very offensive** to do this to **a person,** because it's usually used on **dogs.**

Raising your arm with your palm facing you means **"thank you"** in Mexico.

Placing your **finger** into your **cheek** means **"delicious!"** in Italy.

Making **two fists with your thumbs tucked inside** and hitting them gently on something means **"Good Luck!"** in **Germany** and **Austria**.

In the UK, **tapping your nose** in means something is **confidential**, but in Italy, it means **"watch out"**. In **Japan**, pointing at **your nose** is a way of **referring to yourself**.

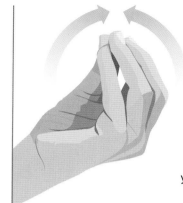

Pinching your fingers together means different things in different countries. In **Italy**, it asks **"What's this?"** or **"What do you want?"** In **Turkey**, it means something is **beautiful** or **good**. In the **Democratic Republic of Congo** it represents a **small amount** of something. And in **Egypt** it shows you will **be ready very soon**.

In **Ghana,** if you pat your **stomach** with your **right hand** and then **raise** it, it means you are **satisfied**.

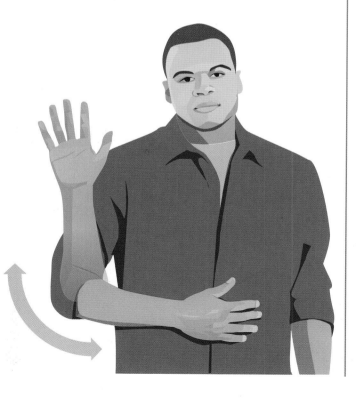

Counting to five around the world:

UK and North America

Europe

Japan

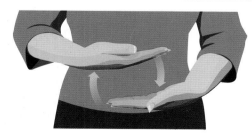

To say **"I don't believe you"** in **France**, use your **index finger** to touch beneath your **eye**.

In **Brazil**, slapping your fingers against your other hand, then swapping hands and slapping again means **"I don't care"**.

153

Out of this world

The image of **the world** being **carried through space** on the back of a **"Cosmic Turtle"** may seem unusual, but this idea appears in **Indian**, Chinese, and **Native American** mythology.

Before the world had been fully explored, **medieval mapmakers** would draw pictures of **sea monsters** or **dragons** in uncharted areas – to warn of the **dangers** that might lurk there.

The myth of the **lost city of Atlantis**, that is said to have disappeared **under the sea**, may have its basis in fact. It could have been destroyed by a **volcanic explosion** 3,600 years ago.

The knowledge that **Earth is a globe** has been around since the 6th century BCE, but **flat Earth** remained a competing theory. When ancient Greek philosopher **Herodotus** mapped the world in 500 BCE, he showed it as flat and with Greece at the centre!

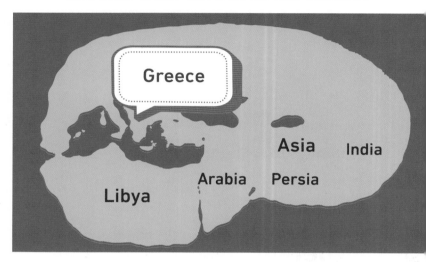

Greece

Asia

India

Arabia

Persia

Libya

Oceans make up **71 per cent** of Earth's surface, so if **aliens** ever **visited**, they would probably **land in the sea**.

Many cultures imagined **the dead** lived in an **underworld** below Earth. **The Mayans** believed that this cave in Belize led to their underworld **"Xibalba"**.

Ancient **Greek astronomer Ptolemy** (100–170 CE) started the popular early theory that everything in the **Universe** – the **Sun**, other stars, and **planets** – **revolved** around **Earth**.

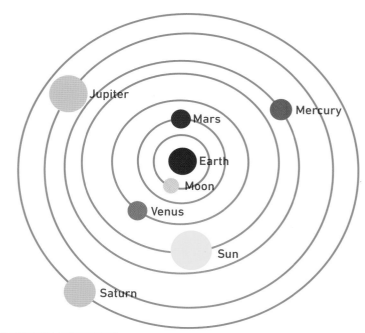

Ancient Greek mathematician **Eratosthenes** measured the **size of Earth** as far back as 240 BCE. The answer he got – **40,000 km** (25,000 miles) – was almost exactly right.

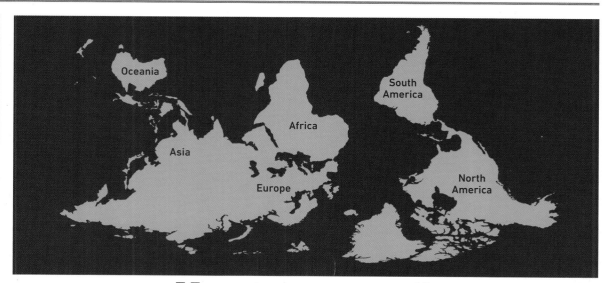

More than 1,000 years later, when **Galileo Galilei** tried to argue **Earth** revolved around the **Sun**, the Catholic church put him **on trial**, and locked him up under **house arrest**!

Ever since ancient times, some people have argued **Earth is hollow**. It has been suggested to contain a **fiery chasm**, a network of **caverns**, or even a series of **smaller globes**.

Which way is up? **Maps** normally put **north** at the top, but **Earth** is a **rotating sphere**, so has no "up" or "down".

Index

Acknowledgements

Dorling Kindersley would like to thank: Hazel Beynon for proofreading, Carron Brown for indexing, and Ann Baggaley, Jessica Cawthra, Anna Fischel, Anna Limerick, and Georgina Palfrey for additional editorial work.

The publisher would like to thank the following for their kind permission to reproduce their photographs:

(Key: a-above; b-below/bottom; c-centre; f-far; l-left; r-right; t-top)

1 123RF.com: Elena Schweitzer (tc). **TurboSquid:** 3d_molier International (bc) **2 Alamy Stock Photo:** World History Archive (tr). **Rex Shutterstock:** Shaun Jeffers (tc) **3 123RF.com:** Chris Boswell (tc). **Alamy Stock Photo:** imageBROKER (tl); mauritius images GmbH (tc/Tomato Festival); Nature Picture Library (tr) **4-5 Rex Shutterstock:** Shaun Jeffers **6 Alamy Stock Photo:** lynn hilton (tr). **Dreamstime.com:** Nahiluoh (cb). **Getty Images:** Allentown Morning Call (tc); Speleoresearch & Films / Carsten Peter (ca); robertharding / Lee Frost (crb). **iStockphoto.com:** Vadim_Nefedov (clb); Virginia44 (tl). **Andrés Ruzo:** (c) **7 123RF.com:** long10000 (cra); Aleksandr Penin (ca); ostill (cr). **iStockphoto.com:** guenterguni (cl); mazzzur (c). **Professor J. Colin Murrell:** (tl). **Jordan Westerhuis:** (crb) **8 123RF.com:** konstantin32 (bl); Petr Podrouzek (clb). **Depositphotos Inc:** frankix (cb); sellphoto1 (bc). **Dreamstime.com:** Bcbounders (cl); Bennymarty (c) **10 Alamy Stock Photo:** Aurora Photos (bl) **11 123RF.com:** lightpoet (tr). **Alamy Stock Photo:** Roger Coulam (tc); gadag (tl) **15 iStockphoto.com:** narloch-liberra (br) **17 Getty Images:** Julia Cumes (tc) **18 123RF.com:** belikova (cb); Konstantin Kopachinsky (cr); lorcel (tc). **Alamy Stock Photo:** Joan Gil (tr); HI / Gunter Marx (ca). **Dreamstime.com:** Anna Krasnopeeva (cra). **Getty Images:** EyeEm / Patrick Walsh (cla). **iStockphoto.com:** Jose carlos Zapata flores (c) **19 123RF.com:** Wiesław Jarek (ftl); Alessandro Ghezzi (bc/Kaihalulu); iriana88w (fcr); Olga Khoroshunova (c); Phurinee Chinakathum (tr). **Alamy Stock Photo:** Arterra Picture Library (bc); FRIEDRICHSMEIER (tl). **Dreamstime.com:** Hupeng (tc); Konart (cr); Patryk Kosmider (bl). **Getty Images:** Alasdair Turner (fbr) **20-21 TurboSquid:** Ultar3d (ducks) **20 TurboSquid:** Sezar1 (c) **21 Rachael Grady:** (tr) **22 123RF.com:** Mirosław Kijewski (ca); vilainecrevette (cra); Sutisa Kangvansap (bc). **Alamy Stock Photo:** John Cancalosi (c); Image Quest Marine (fclb); WILDLIFE GmbH (br); imageBROKER (fcrb). **Ardea:** Science Source / John W. Bova (cla). **DK Images:** Thomas Marent (fcla, cb). **Dreamstime.com:** Whitcomberd (cl). **FLPA:** Minden Pictures / Chien Lee (fcl). **naturepl.com:** Alex Hyde (fcra) **23 123RF.com:** Matee Nuserm (cla, c). **Alamy Stock Photo:** Arco Images GmbH (crb); Lisa Moore (fclb); Stuart Cooper (ca). **Depositphotos Inc:** ead72 (cr). **Dorling Kindersley:** Dreamstime.com: Seatraveler (cl). **Dreamstime.com:** Andrew Astbury (tl); Ethan Daniels (fcr); Marc Witte (fcrb). **FLPA:** Minden Pictures / Chien Lee (clb). **naturepl.com:** PREMAPHOTOS (cra) **25 Dorling Kindersley:** Dreamstime.com: Mgkuijpers (tc); Dreamstime.com: Velora / Anna Bakulina (tr). **iStockphoto.com:** Studio-Annika (tc/Harlequin poison dart frog) **26 Alamy Stock Photo:** Nature Picture Library (tl, clb, cra); Solvin Zankl (br/ Lanternfish, c). **Depositphotos Inc:** stephstarr9363@gmail.com (cla, tr). **Getty Images:** Peter David (fcrb); Joel Sartore (crb). **SuperStock:** Pantheon / Steve Downeranth (cb) **27 Alamy Stock Photo:** blickwinkel (tl); National Geographic Creative (tr); WaterFrame (cr). **Depositphotos Inc:** Fireflyphoto (tc/ Synchronous fireflies). **Getty Images:** Matt Meadows (ftr); Brian J. Skerry (cra); Westend61 (cb) **28 123RF.com:** Andrea Izzotti (bc/crab). **Alamy Stock Photo:** Brandon Cole Marine Photography (bc); Andrey Nekrasov (br) **30 123RF.com:** Natalia Bachkova (br) **31 Alamy Stock Photo:** Premaphotos (bc). **SuperStock:** Minden Pictures / Cyril Ruoso (tc) **33 Alamy Stock Photo:** Nature Picture Library (tr) **34 Alamy Stock Photo:** Frans Lanting Studio (cl) **35 Alamy Stock Photo:** Gianni Muratore (cr) **36 Alamy Stock Photo:** imageBROKER (tr); robertharding (fcl); Darby Sawchuk (tl). **Depositphotos Inc:** casadaphoto (cb); javarman (clb). **Dreamstime.com:** Byelikova (cr); Evgeniefimenko (c). **iStockphoto.com:** drferry (cl) **37 123RF.com:** Dr Ajay Kumar Singh (fcl). **Alamy Stock Photo:** 42pix Premier (br); Patti McConville (bc); Brian McGuire (tr). **Depositphotos Inc:** avk78 (clb); javarman (cl); sainaniritu (fcrb). **Dreamstime.com:** Leslie Clary (c); Florentiafree (tl); Mark Higgins (crb). **iStockphoto.com:** Komngui (cr) **38 iStockphoto.com:** MirekKijewski (bc, br) **39 Depositphotos Inc:** Juan_G_Aunion (cr). **naturepl.com:** MYN / John Tiddy (cra) **40 FLPA:** Steve Gettle / Minden Pictures (crb) **41 Alamy Stock Photo:** Thailand Wildlife (tr) **42-43 Alamy Stock Photo:** World History Archive **44 iStockphoto.com:** xbrchx (br) **45 123RF.com:** hecke (bc). **iStockphoto.com:** BeholdingEye (tc) **47 Alamy Stock Photo:** AF archive (tr). **TurboSquid:** 3d_molier International (tc). **48 Getty Images:** Popperfoto (br) **49 Alamy Stock Photo:** Andrew O'Brien (tc). **Dreamstime.com:** Sergio Boccardo (tr); Conceptw (tc/drone). **iStockphoto.com:** icholakov (tl) **50 Alamy Stock Photo:** Granger Historical Picture Archive (tl) **51 Getty Images:** Tim Graham (tr) **52-53 Wikipedia:** Grumman Tbm Avenger by helijah is licensed under CC Attribution (aircraft) **52 Getty Images:** The LIFE Picture Collection (bc) **53 Alamy Stock Photo:** Kevin Foy (cra). **iStockphoto.com:** Mark_Doh (cr); NejroN (crb) **54 Alamy Stock Photo:** Ken Welsh (bc) **55 Alamy Stock Photo:** Newscom (tc). **Fleur Star:** (bl) **56-57 Dreamstime.com:** Bert Folsom (Basemap) **56 Getty Images:** Klaus Leidorf / Klaus Leidorf / Corbis (br); Hulton Archive (crb) **57 Alamy Stock Photo:** Granger Historical Picture Archive (tr). **Getty Images:** Glenn Hill (tc) **58 Getty Images:** Marka (br) **59 Alamy Stock Photo:** Chronicle (tl) **60-61 Alamy Stock Photo:**imageBROKER **62 Getty Images:** Bettmann (br) **63 Alamy Stock Photo:** ITAR-TASS Photo Agency (tr) **64 Alamy Stock Photo:** Ian Dagnall (cla) **65 iStockphoto.com:** sborisov (br) **66-67 123RF.com:** Alexander Tkach (Basemap) **66 Alamy Stock Photo:** Pep Roig (br) **67 123RF.com:** Israel Horga Garcia (cr). **Getty Images:** VCG (bc) **68 Dreamstime.com:** Mikhail Lavrenov (bl) **71 Depositphotos Inc:** kossarev56@mail.ru (tc). **Getty Images:** The Asahi Shimbun (tr) **72 Getty Images:** Gordon Wiltsie (crb) **72-73 123RF.com:** byzonda (Flame Icons) **73 Getty Images:** MCT (tr) **74 Rex Shutterstock:** Marc Henauer / Solent News (tc) **75 Alamy Stock Photo:** Sabina Radu (bc); Visual&Written SL (cr). **Dreamstime.com:** Topdeq (bl) **76 Alamy Stock Photo:** BRIAN HARRIS (cl); Hemis (bl) **77 123RF.com:** Matyas Rehak (c/Nazca Lines). **Alamy Stock Photo:** Design Pics Inc (c). **Dreamstime.com:** Irissa (tc). **Getty Images:** DEA / A. DAGLI ORTI (cr); Bethany Clarke / Stringer (bl); PIOTR NOWAK / Stringer (bc) **78-79 TurboSquid:** 3dlattest (clapper board); 3d_molier International (OpenBook); Tornado Studio (Classic Book Standing) **78 Alamy Stock Photo:** Endless Travel (br) **79 123RF.com:** Stephan Scherhag (br). **Alamy Stock Photo:** Hilary Morgan (crb). **Dreamstime.com:** Naumenkoaleksandr (bc) **80 123RF.com:** Veronika Galkina (tc); zhaojiankangphoto (fcra); server (c); Saidin B Jusoh (cr). **Alamy Stock Photo:** Boyd Norton (tr); robertharding (cl); Petr Svarc (bc). **Depositphotos Inc:** sborisov (cla). **Dreamstime.com:** Nadezhda Bolotina (cra); Serhii Liakhevych (ca); Volodymyr Dubovets (fcr) **81 123RF.com:** Sergii Broshevan (c). **Alamy Stock Photo:** Tiago Fernandez (cb). **Dreamstime.com:** Cosmopol (crb); Mikepratt (ca/Moraine). **Getty Images:** Jean-Erick PASQUIER (tl). **Science Photo Library:** DR JUERG ALEAN (ca) **82 Getty Images:** UniversalImagesGroup (br) **83 Alamy Stock Photo:** dpa picture alliance (bc) **84 Alamy Stock Photo:** robertharding (bc). **Getty Images:** Universal History Archive (bl) **85 Alamy Stock Photo:** imageBROKER (bc) **86 TurboSquid:** Nestop (Ladder) **89 Alamy Stock Photo:** Pictorial Press Ltd (cr) **91 Science Photo Library:** MARK GARLICK (bc) **92-93 Alamy Stock Photo:** mauritius images GmbH **95 Getty Images:** STRDEL / Stringer (bc) **96 Alamy Stock Photo:** INTERFOTO (tl) **98 Depositphotos Inc:** bit245 (cl); jochenschneider (tl); oksixx (tc, ca); elenathewise (cla); ttatty (c) **99 Alamy Stock Photo:** ASK Images (bc) **101 Alamy Stock Photo:** Pulsar Imagens (bl). **Depositphotos Inc:** smaglov (tc) **102 Alamy Stock Photo:** Aflo Co. Ltd. (clb) **103 Alamy Stock Photo:** Image Quest Marine (tr); Adrian Sherratt (tc) **104 Alamy Stock Photo:** Nick Gammon (br). **Dreamstime.com:** Kathy Burns (cl). **Getty Images:** Robert Frerck (bl); Philip Gould (tl) **104-105 Alamy Stock Photo:** Piter Lenk (Basemap) **105 Alamy Stock Photo:** ZUMA Press, Inc. (br). **Getty Images:** Barcroft Media (tr); Jeff J Mitchell / Staff (tl); Chung Sung-Jun / Staff (cr) **106 Alamy Stock Photo:** Pete Lusabia (br) **107 Alamy Stock Photo:** WENN Ltd (tc) **108 Alamy Stock Photo:** DavidDent (cla); imageBROKER (cl); Philip Mugridge (clb) **109 123RF.com:** Fabian Ploc (tr). **Alamy Stock Photo:** David Wall (crb). **Dreamstime.com:** Freelady (cr) **110 iStockphoto.com:** Mumemories (crb) **112 Dreamstime.com:** Icononiac (br) **113 Depositphotos Inc:** paulobaqueta (bc). **iStockphoto.com:** zhuzhu (bl) **114 Rex Shutterstock:** Sipa Press (br)**116-117 Dorling Kindersley:** *Metalmorphosis* reproduced with the kind permission of David Cerny; *Ballerina Clown* reproduced by kind permission of Jonathan Borofsky; *Possanka* reproduced with the kind permission of Alvar Gullichsen. **116 Alamy Stock Photo:** Xinhua (bl). **Dreamstime.com:** Ykartsova (br) **118-119 Dreamstime.com:** Seamartini (Basemap) **118 Getty Images:** Paula Bronstein (br) **119 Alamy Stock Phot** ITAR-TASS Photo Agency (bl) **121 Alamy Stock Photo:** jeremy sutton-hibbert (tr). **Getty Images:** Ian Cook (bc) **122-123 123RF com:** Chris Boswell **124 Dreamstime.com:** Yulan (bl) **125 iStockphoto.com:** Benkrut (tr **126 123RF.com:** Chris Boswell (tl); ricochet64 (fcra); snehit (cla); Jesse Kraft (cb). **Alamy Stock Photo:** Panther Media GmbH (cl); redbrickstock.com (crb); tropicalpix / JS Callahan (cr). **Depositphotos Inc:** Zunek (c). **Dreamstime.com:** Lee O'dell (cla/Bannack) **127 123RF.com:** bloodua (tl); motive56 (cra); milla74 (fcla); pytyczech (fclb). **Alamy Stock Photo:** ITAR-TASS Photo Agency (cla); Paul Mayall Australia (crb); Ka Kallou (cr); Pradeep Soman (c); Jim Keir (cl **Getty Images:** Carl Court (bc). **iStockphoto. com:** andzher (tr) **129 The Museum of Army Flying:** (bl) **130 Alamy Stock Photo:** Science History Images (br) **132 Alamy Stock Photo** Everett Collection Inc (crb) **133 Alamy Stock Photo:** Art Collection 2 (tr) **134 Alamy Stock Photo:** Art Collection 2 (br) **135 Alamy Stock Photo:** World History Archive (tr) **136-137 Alamy Stock Photo:** Nature Picture Library **138 Alamy Stock Photo:** Francis Vachon (tr) **Depositphotos Inc:** jovannig (bl). **Dreamstime.com:** Sashkinw (crb) **139 Depositphotos Inc:** flocutus (tr) **140 Depositphotos Inc:** DanFLCreativo (cr). **Getty Images:** The Washington Post (tl) **141 Depositphotos Inc:** pxhidalgo (cl) **142 Depositphotos Inc:** demerzel21 (bl). **Getty Images:** Martin Harvey (cr) **143 Depositphotos Inc:** czamfir (br); ThomasAmby (cl) **146 Depositphotos Inc:** THPStock (tl). **Getty Images:** Henna Malik (br) **147 Getty Images:** MANJUNATH KIRAN Stringer (br) **148 Depositphotos Inc:** sumners (tl). **NASA:** MSFC (br) **149 Depositphotos Inc:** brians101 (t) **150 Depositphotos Inc:** anekoho (t) **151 Depositphotos Inc:** diktattoor (br); Dirima (tc); yayayoyo (bc) **154 123RF.com:** Elena Schweitzer (cr). **Alamy Stock Photo:** Semen Tiunov (tl). **155 Alamy Stock Photo:** National Geographic Creative (tl).

All other images © Dorling Kindersley
For further information see: **www.dkimages.com**

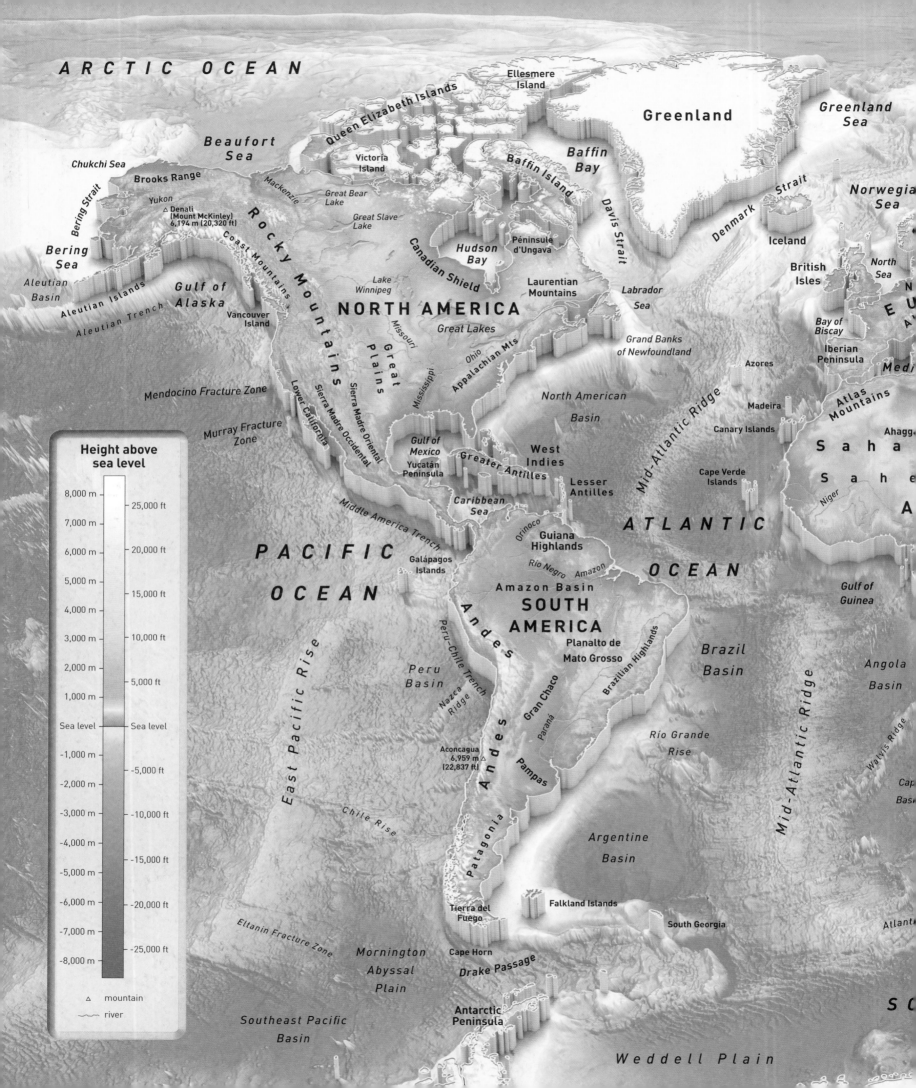

ARCTIC OCEAN

Chukchi Sea
Beaufort Sea
Queen Elizabeth Islands
Ellesmere Island
Greenland
Greenland Sea

Brooks Range
Victoria Island
Baffin Island
Baffin Bay
Norwegian Sea

Bering Strait
Yukon
Mackenzie
Great Bear Lake
Péninsule d'Ungava
Denmark Strait
Iceland

△ Denali
(Mount McKinley)
6,194 m (20,320 ft)
Great Slave Lake
Hudson Bay
Davis Strait
British Isles
North Sea
EU

Bering Sea
Canadian Shield
Laurentian Mountains
Labrador Sea
Bay of Biscay

Aleutian Basin
Gulf of Alaska
Lake Winnipeg
NORTH AMERICA
Iberian Peninsula
Medi

Aleutian Islands
Vancouver Island
Great Lakes
Grand Banks of Newfoundland
Azores

Aleutian Trench
Coast Mountains
Rocky Mountains
Missouri
Ohio
Appalachian Mts
North American Basin
Madeira
Atlas Mountains
Saha

Mendocino Fracture Zone
Great Plains
Mississippi
Canary Islands
Sahel

Murray Fracture Zone
Lower California
Sierra Madre Occidental
Sierra Madre Oriental
Gulf of Mexico
Greater Antilles
West Indies
Mid-Atlantic Ridge
Cape Verde Islands
Niger
Ahagg

Middle America Trench
Yucatán Peninsula
Lesser Antilles
ATLANTIC

PACIFIC OCEAN
Galápagos Islands
Caribbean Sea
OCEAN
Gulf of Guinea

Orinoco
Guiana Highlands

East Pacific Rise
Río Negro
Amazon

Peru-Chile Trench
Amazon Basin
SOUTH AMERICA
Brazil Basin
Angola Basin

Peru Basin
Nazca Ridge
Andes
Planalto de Mato Grosso
Brazilian Highlands
Río Grande Rise
Mid-Atlantic Ridge

Aconcagua
6,959 m
(22,837 ft)
Gran Chaco
Paraná
Walvis Ridge

Chile Rise
Pampas
Argentine Basin
Cap
Bas

Patagonia
Atlan

Eltanin Fracture Zone
Tierra del Fuego
Falkland Islands
South Georgia

Mornington Abyssal Plain
Cape Horn
Drake Passage
SO

Southeast Pacific Basin
Antarctic Peninsula

Weddell Plain

Height above sea level

8,000 m	
	25,000 ft
7,000 m	
	20,000 ft
6,000 m	
5,000 m	15,000 ft
4,000 m	
3,000 m	10,000 ft
2,000 m	
1,000 m	5,000 ft
Sea level	Sea level
-1,000 m	-5,000 ft
-2,000 m	
-3,000 m	-10,000 ft
-4,000 m	
-5,000 m	-15,000 ft
-6,000 m	
-7,000 m	-20,000 ft
-8,000 m	-25,000 ft

△ mountain
river